I
Took the
Only Path
To See You

A Guide to
Finding
Professional
Success
Without
Sacrificing
Personal
Happiness

I
Took the
Only Path
To See You

Jon Fisher
with Gerald Fisher
and Wallace Wang

WILEY

Published by John Wiley & Sons, Inc., Hoboken, New Jersey.
Published simultaneously in Canada.

For general information on our other products and services or for technical support, please contact our Customer Care Department within the United States at (800) 762-2974, outside the United States at (317) 572-3993 or fax (317) 572-4002.

Wiley publishes in a variety of print and electronic formats and by print-on-demand. Some material included with standard print versions of this book may not be included in ebooks or in print-on-demand. If this book refers to media such as a CD or DVD that is not included in the version you purchased, you may download this material at http://booksupport.wiley.com. For more information about Wiley products, visit www.wiley.com.

Library of Congress Cataloging-in-Publication Data

Names: Fisher, Jon B., 1972- author. | Fisher, Gerald A. (Gerald Allen),
   author. | Wang, Wally, author.
Title: I took the only path to see you : a guide to finding professional
   success without sacrificing personal happiness / Jon Fisher with Gerald
   Fisher and Wallace Wang.
Description: Hoboken, New Jersey : Wiley, [2021]
Identifiers: LCCN 2021028063 (print) | LCCN 2021028064 (ebook) | ISBN
   9781119790204 (cloth) | ISBN 9781119790259 (adobe pdf) | ISBN
   9781119790228 (epub)
Subjects: LCSH: Work-life balance. | Success in business.
Classification: LCC HD4904.25 .F54 2021 (print) | LCC HD4904.25 (ebook) |
   DDC 650.1—dc23
LC record available at https://lccn.loc.gov/2021028063
LC ebook record available at https://lccn.loc.gov/2021028064

Cover Design: C. Wallace
Author Photo: Frankie Frost

SKY10028662_080321

To my sister, Danielle

Our childhood relationship may have been rocky, and sometimes it still is now, but often "rocks" make for wonderful cocktails.

CONTENTS

THE TALE OF TWO WOLVES

One evening, an old Cherokee told his grandson about a battle that goes on inside people. He said, "My son, the battle is between two 'wolves' inside us all.

"One is Evil. It is anger, envy, jealousy, doubt, sorrow, regret, greed, arrogance, self-pity, guilt, resentment, inferiority, lies, false pride, superiority, and ego."

"The other is Good. It is joy, peace, love, hope, serenity, humility, kindness, benevolence, empathy, generosity, forgiveness, truth, compassion and faith."

The grandson thought about it for a minute and then asked his grandfather: "Which wolf wins?"

The old Cherokee simply replied, "The one you feed."

PREFACE

UNIVERSITY OF SAN FRANCISCO COMMENCEMENT SPEECH 2018

Thank you very much. My father's commencement speaker was the great Martin Luther King.

My Father was 20 years old and didn't show up for that talk, so thank you for showing up! Thank you, Dean Davis, President Fitzgerald, my friend Dr. Mark Cannice, the rest of the distinguished faculty and invited guests, the families, especially the parents, especially the parents who labored to get here financially, medically . . . emotionally . . . and can I get an Amen for the University of San Francisco graduates! I'm honored you graduates would spend such a special moment of your lives with me.

Of course you didn't really have a choice. I was President Fitzgerald's decision – a decision by a man who has lived, studied, and worked all over the world including Germany, France, Switzerland, Mexico, China, and Kenya and who decided I was the one for you to listen to before getting your diplomas.

Really? This is a question some of those parents who labored to get here may be asking themselves. I mean c'mon, there are three other Jon Fishers to choose from in the Bay Area alone, and all of them are billionaires!

If it's any consolation, I don't think President Fitzgerald was simply inspired in his choice. Some of you graduates attended my lectures at USF – I haunted this university for the last decade banging my fist on chalkboards and desks – pleading with you guys, as you started your projects, your companies, your careers, to marry the right person. To me, this was the most important decision in my life with the most effect on future happiness.

The most traditionally successful people I know were very often divorced, and they told me sacrificing their families wasn't worth it. Who you marry determines the children you may have. Hold your children up high as your greatest inventions, because, to me, they are.

I invented something many of you use every day, and it doesn't compare to any day with a happy, healthy child.

Don't step on anyone's neck to advance your cause. Be a kind person. Never sue anyone and try not to get sued – you will sleep better at night. I have never been a party to a lawsuit in my technology career and Amen to that!

My wife and I don't put work before our daughter or each other. The engineers in my company, with similar families, and I have been together for most of our professional lives. We don't waste time commuting to offices to look over shoulders because we trust each other.

We don't have a holiday party. We don't have each other over for dinner. We get it done, then we see our families.

We're like a less good-looking, legal, married-with-children version of the *Ocean's Eleven* team.

We build good companies that great companies buy and take around the world as our path of least resistance to contributing to the world. Building smaller companies takes a lot less capital and therefore a lot less risk, and therefore less of a personal toll. And this works in other industries – financially, my companies look a lot like Seth Rogen's movies – a strict budget, an acceptably sized audience, although much smaller than a blockbuster. He seems like a pretty happy guy, too.

I accepted President Fitzgerald's invitation because I think you can hear the siren call in your lives without it leading to you crashing against the rocks, and I think that's worth sharing.

Not everything in Silicon Valley, or any industry or life for that matter, need be portrayed as home runs or strikeouts – success or failure – it's just what you hear about so often because it's what sells newspapers.

You can have an idea that doesn't yield a better way to do your job or give rise to a new company but changes your life. What's that worth? Everything, in my book.

I agreed to join my primary school board that changed my life. I learned about parenting and education and philanthropy and what motivates people. I learned more about all kinds of things that made me a better person, husband, and father. You could give some time to charities or church groups or political causes, and feel the growth that comes with pitching in and doing things for others. It will change you in ways that you cannot foresee, but will enrich your life.

Maybe you'll have an idea about attacking global warming. We sure need them at this time in Earth's history. Maybe you'll have an idea about overcoming racial hatred or poverty, or truth in news reporting, and maybe you'll pursue none of those things, and yet except you'll speak from your heart about them to inspire the person you're going to marry.

I had the idea to give this speech exactly seven years ago to the day. I sat in this church right there. It was December 14, 2012; that was the day all those children were lost in the Sandy Hook shooting. I wondered what someone standing up here would say to us that day and then I wondered what I would to say to you that day. I thought in an increasingly unrecognizable world – my life trajectory should be recognizable to you.

You can do it. You can do what I've done. That is, you can be happy in your career and family

And if you want the world to know your name and you're willing to risk it all to get there, I applaud you, really, and I wish you every success – just remember my name as your backup plan.

I do hope you return to Saint Ignatius once in a while, as I have. Although I was not brought up with religious affiliation, empty churches always give me a sense of peace and motivation to do right in this world. I always walked out of this church on a hill feeling better – even on that Sandy Hook day – feeling at the center of things.

Salesforce built the greatest skyscraper in the land just two miles from here for a reason. It was in San Francisco where my father taught physics at both San Francisco State and Stanford, and often it was easier to get the great physicists of the century to speak in San Francisco. This place stimulates drive and achievement.

About 80 percent of you graduating today do not call San Francisco your home city, but more of you will stay. You understand the feeling I am describing in your years here. San Francisco is a unique city in many ways, and you were lucky to have been here. Bring its vibe wherever you go.

Returning again today, I know the opportunity to speak to you in this place and time may be my apex at age 46 for a variety of reasons, including both sets of parents are still relatively happy and healthy and get to be a part of this. My family is here today. My mother-in-law is here, who believes all of this – career, family, inspiration, all of it, is due to grand design. My mother believes this is all due to chance. I think it's somewhere in the middle.

By the way, this was also the exact opening of my wedding vows. I continued, promising my wife that I would meet her in the middle of our disagreements, whether or not they were about our mothers. And while I think having a loving family creates memorable moments that may result in chemical changes in the brain to make us more creative, I think we should also follow Jack Warner's advice to Einstein, paraphrasing "you have your theory of relatively and I have mine – don't hire a relative."

I have a house on a hill now that's built into a cliff – into the rock. "And the rain fell, and the floods came, and the winds blew and beat on that house, but it did not fall . . ." Matthew 7:24. And Amen to that. The house will not fall, and I remember that to give me strength when bad things happen, which they inevitably do. I am a human, not a house, but still . . .

I see these guys eulogizing their fathers from time to time on CNN, and it's so tough not to cry, and my own father is right here. And he is, not was, a great father. He's really a good guy, you know? I aspire to that. I aspire to that first before anything else.

And my mother is great – she literally stood in front of me to protect from the world at times.

And my wife – I couldn't have imagined winding up with such a loving and patient and good person in my life like her mother. And it is with such humility that I witness all of this passed down to our little girl. Maybe you'll see her at the reception – she shines. I took the only path to see you along Tiburon Blvd, where some of the most well-meaning and resourceful people in town can't seem to change daily driving habits to fix the traffic problem. My daughter and I ride an electric tandem bicycle to her school. I may get funny looks from passing drivers, but we try to do our bit to be environmentally correct. No worry.

So it is in most towns. How do we do what has to be done to save the planet if we can't even sacrifice a little? My daughter's future depends on a healthy planet, and I will work as hard as I can to make it happen for her and future generations. Love may be the greatest motivation we humans have, greater than success or money.

The Union of Concerned Scientists just forecasted that nearly 4,400 homes in Marin County will be underwater in less than 30 years because of sea level rise, so we'll have to do something. My generation, yours, we will have to do something. For now, I keep searching for ideas. Think about these things. Ideas will come to you, and act to make this a better planet. Together, we can make it happen. Angry and divided, I fear we cannot.

We named our daughter after Emerson, who wrote, "Do not go where the path may lead, go instead where there is no path, and leave a trail." What a trail to leave, a healthy Earth and good will among men (and woman).

Your degrees today and your work to come are the means to leave a trail. Your family is another. I will look for you in this church in the years to come as you build and find your happiness.

Thank you USF and Go Dons!

INTRODUCTION

O ur country is not doing well. In the last several years, intense negative emotions such as hate, fear, resentment, and distrust have dominated the headline news. Toss in problems from pandemics and politicians fighting over scientific facts and we have a divided, often dysfunctional society. This makes effective action to combat global warming, job loss, economic stagnation, virus outbreaks, and other threats next to impossible.

To reverse this negative and dangerous trend, we will need a social revolution. People don't necessarily need to love their neighbor, but they should at least respect their neighbors through simple acts of consideration, kindness, and even compassion.

When someone receives respect and compassion, life can change dramatically in an instant – for both the recipient and the sender. Caring can spread quickly and be just as contagious as a disease, but in a good way. Ultimately, this spreading of kindness can create a society that can act and work together for the common good.

The USA should become the United States of Affiliation, not Antipathy. This needed social revolution may take time to counteract the negative forces omnipresent today, but that's the reason for this book. This book is my way to help the process along and make the world a better place for everybody.

Inside, you'll read about people I personally know or have heard about from the people closest to me. Many of these people are famous and household names, like President Joe Biden, whom I first met when he visited my company for a pre-election fundraiser. These are troubled times, and Biden seems to understand that coming together can accomplish things that disunity will impede or make impossible. It is too soon to know if he has the magic to do this.

Others I write about are like Larry Ellison of Oracle fame, who bought my software company where I worked as an Oracle executive for a time. His domain was not as large as Biden's, but he built a powerful and lasting company. Some have referred to Ellison as a modern-day Genghis Kahn, but he has certainly done very well for his children financially.

Part of this story includes Nobel Prize winners as part of this story, along with many ordinary people whose stories deserve to be told because they all showed kindness. Their caring provides plenty of evidence that you don't have to be a bastard to succeed. In fact, being a nice person can actually enhance your chances of success.

Kindness and caring only needs to start with one person, and it can spread to many others, one person at a time, crossing international borders and leaping across entire continents and oceans. Caring and kindness can spark the next revolution, because in the end, we are all our brother's keepers. We just need to learn that compassion is never a weakness but a strength, and the best way to learn how to change the world is to see how others have done it first.

CHAPTER 1

The Most Important Choice in the World

Imagine you're a kid in a candy store. Everywhere you look, there's a treat you'd like to try. Paralyzed with indecision, you can only look from side to side, fearing if you choose one candy, you'll miss out on the opportunity to choose another one.

With so many tempting choices, you'd think it should be easy to choose something. After all, if everything looks appealing, how can you possibly lose? Yet there is a way to lose – by being afraid to choose anything. When the candy store owner finally closes the doors, that's when you'll realize you wound up getting nothing, despite being surrounded by everything, all because you couldn't make a decision.

Don't be a kid in a candy store.

You have to make a decision right now that will affect the rest of your life. The longer you procrastinate, the harder your decision will get. You also can't let someone else make this decision for you. It's all on you, yet many people go through their entire lives without making it.

No matter how old you may be, where you live, or what you're currently doing, this decision is vitally important because your life depends on it.

This decision is simple. When will you decide to take charge of your own life?

As straightforward as this question might seem, it's still deceptively difficult. That's why most people avoid answering this question or refuse to acknowledge that it even exists. Yet whether you answer this question or not, your reaction will reveal two important truths.

First, are you willing to take responsibility for your life right now? Once you take responsibility for your life, guess what? You now hold the key to the greatest force in the world, which is nothing more than the power of choice.

You have shaped your life up until this point, which means you also have the power to shape your life differently now and in the future. Sure, what others do in your life matters, but if you're the only one who can control your life, then you can change your life for the better, no matter who may get in your way or what anyone else might say.

Taking responsibility for your life and acknowledging that you're in control automatically removes all excuses. That can be scary but also empowering because that means you can change your life for the better at a moment's notice.

That's true power that no amount of money can buy.

Just as Dorothy in *The Wizard of Oz* finally learned that she had the power to go home at any time, you always have the power to improve your life at any time. Once you acknowledge that you alone hold this power, you'll possess the greatest force in the world, which is the ability to shape the future of your life at any time.

If you don't think you have any control over your life, ask yourself what you could do right now that would make your life infinitely worse. Most likely, you can come up with dozens of ways you can make your life worse than it is right now, but if you can make your life worse, that also means you can also choose ways to make your life better.

Before you can make your life better, you need to believe that's even an option.

Once you know you hold the power to choose between making your life better or making your life worse, you must choose to make your life better. Then you must take action to make your life better. It's that simple.

Remember the three Cs of life: Choices, Chances, and Changes. Until you make a choice to take a chance, your life will never change. As Eleanor Roosevelt said, "I am who I am today because of the choices I made yesterday." Author and motivational speaker Wayne Dyer said, "When you abandon making choices, you enter the vast world of excuses."

Don't make excuses. Start changing your life for the better today. Once you know what you want to change in your life, you can then make a choice. If a choice doesn't quite work out the way you want, you can always make another choice. The power of choice makes you capable of doing anything you want. The most important decision you can ever make is deciding that only you can change your life and you can keep making new choices at any time until your life turns out the way you like.

Will you make mistakes? Of course. Will you run into problems? Yes. Can your choices make your life worse off than if you had done nothing at all? Possibly.

However, if you let these fears stop you from trying, you'll never know what you may be missing. There's a whole new life waiting for you but you need to take that first step based on nothing more than faith that a better world is out there.

That's the power of choice. You must recognize that you, and nobody else, holds this power that can literally control your life. Commit to that one decision now and your life will never be the same again.

I guarantee it.

Takeaway: Acknowledge that you have the power to change your life by making decisions. No matter what your situation may be, you always have the choice to make your life better (or worse) at each moment in time. The more positive choices you make in your life, the greater impact you'll have on your life in the long run.

Portraits in Kindness

By Gerald Fisher

Kindness has been around for my entire life. I just wasn't aware of it until I started doing some research about kindness. I found some colleagues were kind while others were not so kind. That's when I noticed that kindness was an admirable attribute because we all appreciate people who are kind.

Clearly kindness affects us, but I didn't see the bigger picture that kindness could also be contagious and be a major factor in the conduct of business. Not only is it true that you don't have to be a bastard to succeed, but it's also true that if you have a certain kindness in your life and in your spirit, it will affect the people around you and be contagious. Then you'll be even more successful than if you were calculating, nasty, and unkind to others.

The example that pops into my mind is a major quarterback for an NFL team who was well known to everyone. During training camp, there was a rookie trying to make the team's center. So he snapped the ball to the star quarterback, but the ball hit his fingers at an awkward angle and the quarterback winced in pain as the ball flew high in the air.

At this point, the whole coaching staff ran out on the field. Half went to see if their star quarterback was seriously injured, and the other half went to berate the rookie center. They were yelling at him, saying, "How can you think of making the team if you snap a football like that? What kind of a player are you? If you hurt our quarterback, you will never see the field and you'll be gone by tomorrow morning."

At this point, the quarterback came over and said, "No, you're getting it wrong. His was a perfect snap. The fault was mine. I was ill positioned."

The rookie center, as you might guess, was so overwhelmed by what the quarterback did that he said to himself, "I'm gonna play for that guy and I'm going to play my heart out," which is what he did.

That was expected from the rookie center, but the additional factor that I hadn't focused on after all these years is that a lot of players witnessed that event. There was a lot of discussion in the clubhouse, a lot of talk amongst the linemen as the people who support the quarterback, and they all were taken aback at how kind and considerate and generous this guy was, and the whole team just reacted with euphoria.

They gave their all for that quarterback. They did things they didn't think they could do. Although it wasn't all entirely due to the generosity of a quarterback, it played a large role in defining that quarterback's position as a leader for the team.

(continued)

(continued)

Many people have contributed major inventions or founded organizations that have literally changed the world and society for the better. While some of these people have been kind and generous to others, others were not. Ultimately, what matters isn't any admiration or accolades someone receives for their actions but how those actions affect other people both individually and collectively throughout an entire organization.

Back when I was a graduate student, another graduate student named Dick had the idea that our little physics department athletic team could win the all University Intramural Athletic Championship. Now the idea that a bunch of physics graduate students could win a sporting competition sounded like mental illness because the intramural championship had always been won by a fraternity or a club, not by a bunch of graduate students in a physics department.

But Dick was a great administrator and a great manager, and he had an idea. He wanted to find people to represent our team in the lesser events because he knew that competition would be strongest in the most popular events but weakest in the lesser events, and that would give us a chance.

So he found a big, strong kid who could represent us in weightlifting. He recruited my best friend in the physics department to throw horseshoes. Keep in mind that my friend had never thrown a horseshoe in his life, but he volunteered and looked up the rules. Now think how many people enter a horseshoes competition. Two, maybe three? It turned out my friend won and allocated all the points from the horseshoe competition to our team's total.

Of course, the points allocated from horseshoes was not equivalent to the points allocated from baseball, football, or basketball, but it was a start. We competed in weightlifting, horseshoes, badminton, and bicycle racing.

Then one day, Dick burst into my office and said, "Fish," which is what he called me, "You've got to get down to the pool. Grab a bathing suit. We're entered in water polo."

Imagine what it was like wandering through the locker room, asking to borrow a bathing suit. It, of course, didn't work so I had to lay out the big bucks at the gym store for a high-tech speedo.

Not only had I never played water polo before, but I had never even seen a water polo match. I told Dick, "I want to help but I'm not much of a swimmer. There's got to be somebody better."

Dick said, "Well, I'll look around. But we can't forfeit. If you forfeit, you get no points, and there are only two other teams entered. One was a varsity swimming team, which has a number of Olympians on it. By some technicality, the swimming team was free to play water polo. The other team was from the university's water polo team that consisted of players who didn't make the varsity, but they were championship players from high school.

And then there was our team.

Dick said, "We're going to come in third. There's no doubt at that, but we're going to get the points for coming in third, which is a lot of points."

(continued)

(*continued*)

Well, not only did I almost drown – apparently there have no rules in water polo – they also just beat the crap out of me and I couldn't even get out of the pool.

I had to go over to the side and use the steps and somebody had to push me from behind. I fell down like a beached whale and good ol' Dick came over and said, "You guys did great! But I have some bad news for you. That was just the first period."

Had I been able to get up and raise my hand, I would have told Dick a thing or two.

Instead I told him, "Just push me back in the pool." When the score reached 58 to nothing, the referees mercifully called the game, but still granted us the points for third place.

Being a great manager and administrator, Dick looked up records on everybody in the department and everybody in the university, and he found Professor Bill Little.

Bill had come to the university as an assistant professor and quickly became an associate professor before being promoted to a full professor. He became a power in the department, and he was only in his thirties. But what caught Dick's attention was that Bill had been the national champion of Scotland in the pole vault during the Cold War.

Dick approached Professor Bill Little, and Little said he would be glad to help. What Bill neglected to say was that he hadn't touched a pole or done any kind of jumping whatsoever in about 15 or 20 years.

Undaunted on the first day of competition, Bill grabbed a pole and ran down the runway. He planted the pole, went up, but went under the bar instead of over it, and flew off to the side, missed the landing area, and almost killed himself.

We all saw that and we thought if Professor Bill was willing to do that, we thought we all had to do the best we could do as well. Professor Bill's generous act spread through the whole group and we did better than we had any right to do.

Amazingly, we wound up winning the All University Championship. The school athletic director even announced our victory at halftime of the homecoming football game. That started our run of two straight years of championships where the physics department won the All University Championship, beating out all the fraternities, all the clubs, and all the other athletes on campus.

Good old Professor Bill did not win any events and was not going to compete against high school all Americans, and people who were currently running track for the university, but he gave us his all, even though he could have killed himself or gotten himself seriously injured.

That showed me that you don't have to be a calculating loser in order to succeed. Instead, you could show an act of kindness, you could show an act of caring and compassion, and it ends up coming back on you and making your organization that much better.

If you are the head of any group, your group will be better and probably the best it can be if your leadership just includes semblances of kindness.

CHAPTER 2

Understanding Happiness

I want you to be happy. That may sound like a lofty dream or a bad sales pitch, but it's true. The happier people are, the better the world will be for everyone. We already know what happens when the world is full of fear, anger, and hate so it's important to make as many people happy as possible starting with you.

So this book is my way of helping make the world a better place for me and my family, and in the process, for you, your family, and everyone you care about. We're in this together and we can do this together. If you want to be happy, here's a secret.

I can help you.

Most people think I'm happy because I'm an entrepreneur who has started four different companies and sold my third one, Bharosa, to Oracle in 2007 for millions of dollars. Other people think I'm happy because I'm a professor teaching business classes at the University of San Francisco. Yet other people think I'm happy because I wrote the book *Strategic Entrepreneurship: Shattering the Start-Up Entrepreneurial Myth*, which is required reading for the MBA program at several business schools including the University of California, Berkeley. Still others think I must be happy because I'm an inventor with more than one hundred patents to my name.

Yet none of this is important. I'm happy because I'm a husband to a wonderful wife, and a father to a lovable daughter. I'm also a son to my parents, and close friends with numerous people I've had the fortune to know over the years. Take away all my money, all my awards, all my patents, and all my accolades, and guess what? I'd still be happy as a husband devoted to my wife, a father to my daughter, a son to my mother and father, and a good friend to so many people I've met throughout my life.

That's because I've learned that the real riches in life can never be measured by the size of your bank account, the number of people who admire you, or the list of accomplishments you may have achieved. Instead, true wealth comes from a clear understanding of what happiness really means.

UNDERSTANDING HAPPINESS

If everyone wants to be happy, why are so many people unhappy? The answer is simple. Most people never take the time to understand how to be happy. If you don't know how to be happy, how can you possibly be happy? That's like trying to fish without knowing what a fish looks like or where fish even live. If you don't know what a fish is or where to find it, you're never going to catch any. Likewise, if you never understand happiness, you're never going to be happy in more than a superficial way.

People spend more time planning a vacation than they spend deciding what would make them happy. When you don't know what will make you happy, you'll risk searching for happiness anywhere and everywhere. When you do this, chances are extremely good that you'll never find it.

Imagine if you live in New York and you want to move to another city. The smart thing to do would be to decide what type of place you would want to live, then research different parts of the country to see which areas most closely match the criteria you set for yourself. Not only does this take time, it also means defining what's most important to you. Sadly, because of the time and effort required, most people never do this.

Rather than define what they want and then look for a place that provides that, most people will just jump in a car and start driving in whatever direction looks most promising at the moment. Instead of defining criteria for the best place to live for them, they'll just wander from place to place, never quite being happy where they're at but quite never knowing which direction they should go either.

Sound familiar?

The first step to happiness is knowing what you want out of life, just like the first step to traveling anywhere is knowing where you want to go. While this may sound simple, it's actually the hardest step of all. Not only must you imagine a brighter future for yourself, but you must believe it's possible for you to reach it.

If you don't believe your life can be dramatically better, you won't bother pursuing it. If you believe in a brighter future but don't believe you can achieve it, you also won't bother pursuing it.

Taking the first step to happiness involves faith – faith in yourself and faith in the world. Faith means embracing an idea, often with no facts or proof to support it. Yet before you can take that first step, you must have faith, and accepting that unknown can be the hardest step of all.

Deciding what you want involves taking a chance. The moment you imagine a brighter future for yourself, it's far too easy to tell yourself you can't have it, you don't deserve it, you're too young (or too old), you don't have enough education, you don't know how to get it, or you're not good enough for whatever reason.

The biggest obstacle to happiness is none other than yourself. The biggest obstacle in your way isn't your parents, your neighbors, people around you, the economy, the government, or the world you live in. The biggest obstacle in your way is staring at you in the mirror every morning. You are your own worst enemy. Yet, you are also your own best chance – but only if you believe you can do it.

So give yourself permission to dream big, and don't limit your ideas. Remember, it doesn't cost anything to let your imagination run wild, but if you choose puny dreams, you'll risk costing yourself a wonderful life if you had only set your sights bigger.

Think back when you were a kid and you could dream anything you wanted, from becoming the first astronaut on Mars to scoring the winning touchdown in the final seconds of the Super Bowl. Forget about being "practical" or "realistic." Dream big, and don't settle for a watered down, diluted version of your dream. If you knew you absolutely could not fail, what would you want to do? You may never achieve your wildest dreams, but by making an effort, you'll go much farther than if you had never done anything at all.

DREAM BIG

You can never get anywhere by just reading this book, so now's the time to take action. For the next four days, spend at least 10 minutes a day writing down one or more big ideas that you'd like to accomplish in your lifetime. For each day, make your ideas bigger and more outlandish than the previous day's ideas. This will force you to keep expanding your mind on what's possible so you don't limit yourself unnecessarily.

On the fifth day, rearrange your ideas from the one you like the most to the one you like the least. Don't judge your ideas by how much you think you can achieve them. Judge your ideas by how much you really want them. If your ideas don't scare or embarrass you by their audacity, you're not dreaming big enough.

On the sixth day, look over your ideas and ask yourself what type of training and skills you'd need to achieve each dream.

Then ask yourself if you'd be willing to take the time and effort needed to achieve that dream.

For example, many people dream about becoming a movie star. Now ask yourself, would you be willing to take the time to take acting classes and practice acting in your spare time, even if you never made any money at it? Would you be willing to go to countless auditions and face rejection at nearly all of them?

If you're not willing to do something for free for the rest of your life, that means you don't really want to do the work needed to achieve that dream. If you won't do the necessary work for free, you're only looking at the benefits and not the activity. That means you really don't want that dream after all.

Finally on the seventh day, find the one idea that you can't live without. If you can live without a particular idea, then it's just a pleasant fantasy. If you know in your heart that you can't live without a dream, then that's the one dream that you need to pursue the most.

Make sure the dream you pick is one that you want, not something your parents, friends, or relatives want for you. This is your life so you must decide what you truly want, not what you think you should do. It's easy to have a dream but it's much harder to find your passion.

Passion is what you're willing to do for free because you enjoy that particular activity.

Passion is what makes you happy.

Ultimately, passion is what makes life worth living.

Drain a life of passion and you really have no life at all. Tragically, people can go through their whole lives without ever finding their passion. Without passion, it's too easy to get distracted by superficial pleasures like drugs, sex, and alcohol that ultimately never brings lasting happiness. With passion, your life will have purpose, direction, and above all, a sense of meaning.

Ultimately, happiness comes from pursuing your passion. Until you find what you're passionate about, lasting happiness will likely elude you, creating a life of frustration and boredom. However, once you discover your life's passion, you can feel more in control of your world because you'll know what you want and have the courage to go out and get it no matter what obstacles may get in your way.

Passion is the spark of life. Finding what you are passionate about can change your life overnight.

Debbi Fields was only 20 years old when she started selling homemade chocolate cookies. She turned her love for cookies into a multimillion-dollar business as founder of Mrs. Fields Cookies.

Nick Woodman loved surfing, and while surfing along the coast of Australia, he got the idea to develop straps that could hold a camera that could record a surfer's best moments on the waves. Eventually, he decided to create his own wearable camera, and this turned into the GoPro camera that developed into a million-dollar business.

Walt Disney enjoyed drawing and created various animated characters with different animation companies. Although these early characters and animation companies failed, Walt Disney eventually succeeded when he created Mickey Mouse.

At age 15, Greta Thunberg started protesting outside the Swedish parliament to take action on climate change. Her action inspired other students to organize similar strikes for the climate. After addressing the United Nations Climate Change Conference, Greta soon became a popular environmental activist known throughout the planet.

These people aren't successful because they made a lot of money or became famous. They're successful because they pursued their passion, and their passion helped them overcome any

fears, doubts, and obstacles in their way. How happy and successful would Debbi Fields be if she had tried to start an animation
company while Walt Disney tried to bake cookies?

For every Debbi Fields or Walt Disney, there are thousands
of people happily pursuing their passion in all walks of life all
over the world. You may have never heard of these people but
you can recognize them because they've chosen a life they enjoy
every second of the day.

Everyone has a different passion, so the only person who
can discover what your passion might be is you.

Take the time now to decide what you're most passionate
about. If you don't know, stop reading right now. Then spend
however much time you need to find your passion, because if
you don't find it now, it will be too easy to let inertia take over
so you drift through life with no purpose, direction, or meaning
whatsoever. Finding your passion literally defines your life.

The huge difference between passion and fantasy is that
fantasy focuses solely on a goal (and all its benefits), while passion focuses on both a goal and the activity needed to achieve
that goal.

MONEY WILL NEVER MAKE YOU HAPPY

Perhaps the biggest myth that too many people believe is
that money will make them happy. Yet they never define how
much money would make them happy. If you had a dollar more,
would you be happy? A thousand dollars more? A million?
Ten million?

I guarantee that whatever amount of money you think
will make you happy will never be enough because money
alone can never make you happy. People think money will
make them happy, but evidence consistently shows how wrong
that can be.

Many people play the lottery because they fantasize about winning a fortune. Yet the list of multimillion-dollar lottery winners who consistently fail to find happiness is horrifying.

In 2002, construction company owner John Whittaker won $315 million in the Powerball lottery. Yet within five years, he had spent all his money. Even worse, his granddaughter developed a drug habit and died. When asked about his lottery winnings, Whittaker and his wife said if they could go back in time, they'd tear up that lottery ticket.

Evelyn Basehore won $3.9 million playing New Jersey's lottery. Incredibly, she kept playing the lottery and won another $1.4 million. Yet all that money went to relatives and poor investment choices. Then she gambled away the rest of the money in Atlantic City casinos, leaving her broke and forced to live in a trailer park, where she had to work two jobs just to pay her bills.

Abraham Shakespeare won $30 million and suddenly found himself hounded by people who wanted a share of his fortune. Before Shakespeare got murdered by his girlfriend, he told his few remaining friends, "I'd have been better off broke. I thought all these people were my friends, but then I realized all they want is just money."

Still think money can buy happiness?

People want money because they think more money represents freedom. Money does give you more opportunities, but that also means more opportunities to screw up. When people say they want more money, what they're really saying is that they want more material possessions.

Just watch professional athletes who sign multimillion-dollar contracts and rush out to buy three sports cars, two homes, a stable of race horses, and a yacht. Buying objects that you couldn't afford before can be fun, but that enjoyment will only be momentary.

After that initial feeling of euphoria passes, you'll be left searching for happiness all over again. You can only spend so much and buy so many objects before you run out of money and lose track of all the objects you bought. If you can't define a precise dollar amount that will make you happy, that's a big clue that more money will never make you any happier in the long run.

If a doctor said you had one day left to live, what's worth more? A billion dollars or a cure that would keep you alive?

REACHING GOALS ALONE CAN'T MAKE YOU HAPPY

Rather than just wish for more money, some people wish to reach a certain goal in life. That's why so many people dream of becoming A-list movie stars, popular musicians, or famous entrepreneurs. There's nothing wrong with lofty dreams, but what is wrong is thinking that once you reach your goal, you'll achieve happiness.

Read any celebrity news and you'll find plenty of rich, famous people who still aren't happy. The list of popular movie stars and recording artists who died young is tragically long. While some died in accidents, far more died through their own self-destructive behavior, whether through alcohol poisoning, drug overdoses, or outright reckless behavior.

Why do so many celebrities destroy themselves after achieving what they thought would be their greatest dream? Most likely, these celebrities worked their whole lives to achieve fame and success, yet discovered when they finally reached their goals that the happiness they sought for so long had somehow still managed to elude them.

Now what?

Beyond the empty feeling that comes from any disappointment, there's a second problem that comes from striving to reach a goal that you think will bring you happiness. Far too many people make tremendous sacrifices in their lives to reach their dreams, which often means spending less time with friends and family and more time desperately pursuing your dream. When you make that type of trade-off, you've already lost.

Whether you reach your goal or not, living a life without any loved ones will be a lonely existence that can never be replaced with more money to attract fair-weather friends. When you're surrounded by people you barely know with motives that may be highly questionable, all the money and success in the world can't make you feel any less lonely.

If you tie your happiness to becoming a movie star, recording a hit album, or starting a million-dollar company, you'll be highly motivated to do whatever it takes to reach that goal. This intense motivation to succeed can tempt you to sacrifice anything and everything to get it. After all, who wouldn't want to be happy? If you can reach your goal, then it should all be worth it if you can be happy, right?

Wrong.

To achieve their dreams at all costs, people often lie, cheat, and steal. If you have to break the law, violate your own principles, or step on others to get what you want, you can never be a success even if you do achieve your goal.

When you define happiness as a destination to reach, you may justify doing anything to get there. This can't help but create enemies and destroy personal and professional relationships along the way and then what? Reaching a destination, like buying a shiny new toy, may give you a feeling of momentarily happiness, but you must always deal with the consequences afterward.

Ultimately, whether you believe happiness lies in reaching a destination or owning a particular object, you'll be disappointed. Reaching a goal or buying a certain item might make you happy for an instant. Yet after that momentary feeling of euphoria wears off (and it will), you'll risk thinking you just need to get more of the same thing to be happy again, which can start this vicious cycle of no-return all over again.

This is no way to live.

Life can be fun with or without money, success, or fame. I consider myself successful not because of my achievements, who I know, or what I've done, but because I know the two keys to being happy.

First, happiness is never static. That's why you can never achieve lasting happiness just by reaching a goal or buying something you like. Think about a happy moment in your past and you'll realize that happiness is always temporary and fleeting. Happiness isn't an object you can possess but an action you experience. You can never find happiness; you can only create it through action. The moment you stop, happiness disappears.

The type of action that creates happiness is different for everybody because it depends on what you're most passionate about. Author Stephen King spent years working as a janitor, gas pump attendant, and worker in an industrial laundry, but he continued to write because that's what made him happy and gave him hope for a better future. Without his writing to make him happy, Stephen King's early life would have felt desperate and bleak.

Richard Branson got his start publishing a magazine. Later, he used this magazine to advertise record albums that he sold by mail-order. That led to opening his own record store and when that made money, Richard Branson launched the record label Virgin Records, which signed bands that other record labels were reluctant to sign, such as multi-instrumentalist Mike Oldfield (whose debut album, *Tubular Bells*, became a best seller when it was used as the soundtrack for the horror movie classic *The Exorcist*). Branson later signed the controversial band known as the Sex Pistols.

From the money he made with his record label, Branson created his own airline, Virgin Atlantic, and later his own space tourism company, Virgin Galactic. His passion isn't just limited to his initial success in the music industry, but with starting and running businesses that challenge the status quo. No matter how much money he has, Richard Branson simply has fun creating and running businesses. All his money just gives him the freedom to pursue another dream, but even if he didn't have that money, he would still enjoy the activity in starting and running another business even if it's as simple as running a record store.

Many people falsely believe that happiness is something they hope to reach in the distant future. That type of thinking means you can never be happy until the future arrives. If that future never comes, then you risk never being happy.

In contrast, once you find what you like doing, you can start doing it now and be happy today and every day, whether you reach a distant goal in the future or not.

Which way would you rather live?

Second, happiness can only exist through action and relationships. Action means doing anything you're most passionate about. Relationships mean you can only create happiness between yourself and others.

While some people can be perfectly happy in solitude, the majority of people are happiest with friends and loved ones. A 2005 survey from the Pew Research Center found that across different countries and ethnic groups, people reported greater happiness from their marriage than from their careers, community, or wealth. Forty-three percent of married respondents reported that they were "very happy" compared to just 24 percent of single people.

Of course everyone is different, but think about the happiest moments from your own life. Chances are good they involve

shared experiences with others such as celebrating a graduation, going on a first date with the person who would eventually
become your spouse, or just a quiet moment talking with a friend
to share your hopes and dreams.

The reason why all the money, fame, and power in the world
can never make you happy is because life is always better when
you can share it with others. So not only does happiness require
actively doing what you enjoy, but it also involves a shared experienced that can be as simple as picking out a puppy from the
animal shelter or teaching a child how to ride a bicycle for the
first time.

Ever wonder why some poor people are happy and some fab-
ulously wealthy people are miserable? It has nothing to do with
money or possessions but everything to do with doing what you
love and spending time with the people you care about the most.

That's how you create happiness.

- Happiness exists when you're following your greatest passion.
- Happiness occurs when you share a memorable moment
  with someone you care about.

The moment you stop pursuing your passion or separate
from the people you care about the most, happiness goes away
as well. The only way you can bring back happiness is to pursue
your passion and/or share special moments with your loved ones.
It's really that simple.

FINDING HAPPINESS IN YOUR OWN LIFE

Just as you can never get into physical shape by exercising once,
so you can only be happy by constantly following your passion

and spending time with your loved ones. That means you must clearly identify both:

- What is your passion (and how can you pursue it)?
- Who are the most important people in your life (and how can you spend more time with them)?

Until you discover your passion, your life might feel aimless. Of course it's not enough to find your passion. You must also take action to follow through on your passion on a regular basis, every day if possible.

How do you find your passion? First, look for any activity that you enjoy doing. Remember, happiness is an action, not a destination, so you need to find the activity that you enjoy doing as its own reward, regardless of what anyone else might think.

For example, I once met a man who was passionate about spoons. This may sound silly, but he enjoyed spending everyday carving wooden spoons until they resembled sculptures you might expect to find in a museum.

Not only did this man enjoy the activity of carving wood, but he also loved the challenge of carving different items out of wood. He started with spoons but soon branched out to forks, bowls, picture frames, chairs, and anything else that could be shaped out of a single block of wood. His passion was simply carving wood into functional art that you couldn't help but admire.

So you not only want to look for any activity that you enjoy doing regardless of what anyone else might think, but you also want to choose an activity that provides a never-ending challenge. Can you think of a better life than one that lets you spend time doing what you love?

If you already know what you're passionate about, you just need the courage to pursue it and ignore any critics. However, if you're like many people, you may have no idea what you could be passionate about. To help find your passion, look at what you fear.

Far too many people take jobs they don't love because they're too afraid of pursuing what they do love. After all, it's far easier to look for that "safe" and "secure" job that promises a steady income along with the "security" of regular employment.

If you're playing it "safe" in life, ask yourself what are you afraid of? Identifying what you fear can be a huge clue to what you really want to do, but you just don't believe you can do it. Think of fear as a bright red blinking arrow pointing you in the direction you really want to go. Be brave and look past your fear. That's where you'll likely find your true passion in life.

Once you've defined your passion, write it down where you can see it every morning when you wake up. Also, write out your passion – on a piece of paper or on your phone – where you can review it during the day. Finally, study what you're most passionate about right before you go to bed each night. By constantly reminding yourself what you care about most, you can take action every day to move one step closer to your dream until you one day achieve success.

Besides knowing your passion, make a list of the people you care about the most. As much as we try not to face reality, we're all going to die one day, so it's important to spend as much quality time as possible with your loved ones.

That could mean doing something as simple as reading a book to a child before bedtime or riding a bicycle across Europe with a friend over the summer. Think about creating happy moments that you'll always remember with a smile on your face. Realize such moments will become even more precious once you realize we're all getting older and the world keeps changing around us every day. We can only repeat certain moments for a limited amount of time before they're gone for good.

Children grow up, parents get older, friends move away, and jobs change to ensure that life will never stay the same. Remember, everyone's time on Earth is limited and unknown, so make every moment you have as memorable as possible. Happiness is up to you.

CREATE A HAPPINESS SCHEDULE

To get into physical shape, you must follow a regular schedule. Likewise, to find happiness in your life, you must also follow a schedule. If you miss a workout day, you'll feel the difference in your body. If you miss a day without following your passion or being with someone you care about, you'll definitely feel the difference in your emotional state.

Every day, take action pursuing your passion. That action can be as short or as long as you like, but the more time you can spend doing what you love, the happier you'll be.

Use a piece of paper or a scheduling program to block out all necessary activities such as sleeping or going to work or school. Now with the free time remaining, schedule time for yourself.

Time, not money, is the most precious commodity in life. Everyone starts with the same 24 hours every day so spend those 24 hours wisely to follow your passion or share your life with your loved ones.

This is why money, fame, and power really can never make you happy. Once you pursue your dreams and strengthen your relationships with the people closest to you, that's when life becomes most satisfying.

So set aside time every day to follow your passion and be with the people you care about the most. When every day feels special, that's where the true riches in life will be found.

How to Kill Happiness (and How to Get It)

At every moment, you can do something to improve your future. At the same time, you can also do something to hurt your future. By knowing common mistakes people make that can ruin their chances for happiness, you can make sure you don't repeat those same errors in your own life. Remember, the definition of insanity is doing the same thing over and over again and expecting a different result. Here are four myths that threaten future happiness:

1. *You can never find your passion.* If you don't know what you want out of life, you're never going to get it. Without passion, life loses much of its purpose and meaning. Not knowing why you're here can be the most depressing and empty feeling in the world.

2. *You can only find happiness by being selfish.* That makes it far too easy to ignore or even hurt those closest to you. If you're willing to hurt your loved ones in a maniacal pursuit for your own happiness, you'll more than likely hurt others as well. If you ever do reach the goal you're seeking, victory will seem hollow when you have no one around to share your accomplishment. All the gold in the world means nothing to someone stranded on a desert island.

3. *Money will make you happy.* When you pursue money at all costs, it's too easy to do something illegal, unethical, or immoral. Right now as you're reading this book, someone in the world is making money trafficking women and children and getting rich off their suffering. Are you willing to do that just for money?

4. *You can only be happy by reaching a certain goal.* When you focus solely on reaching a goal, you may not enjoy the activity necessary to achieve that particular goal.

If you don't enjoy the necessary tasks and lifestyle changes you need to make to reach that goal, chances are good you'll never reach that goal and you'll actually be miserable in the process.

Even worse, if you're focused on reaching a goal and you don't care about the work needed to reach that goal, you'll be tempted to do whatever it takes to reach that goal. That can mean losing touch with those you care about while hurting acquaintances you meet along the way. Even if you do manage to reach your goal, it can only bring temporary happiness at best, like buying a new car. Do you really want to spend years of your life, engaged in an activity you don't enjoy, just to reach a goal that will fail to make you happy anyway?

If you don't find your passion, you'll just drift through life. Picture hopping in a boat and letting it drift into the Atlantic Ocean. There's a slight chance you might drift toward something wonderful, but there's a much greater chance you'll just drift aimlessly until you die.

If you think money, objects, or goals will make you happy, you'll risk wasting your time chasing an illusion that you might finally reach, only to find that you still aren't happy. Then you'll be right back where you started from.

So here's what you should learn before doing anything else. You don't find happiness, you create it.

You create happiness in two ways. First, by actively pursuing whatever you're passionate about. Second, by spending time with the people you care about the most. You can only create happiness through the action of doing what you love or sharing positive moments with your loved ones where you can help each other, learn from one another, or simply enjoy each other's company.

You find happiness in the active process of doing what you love or being around people who you love. Do this every day and you'll soon have a happy day, a happy week, a happy month, a happy year, and eventually a happy life.

Make a vow to yourself that you'll pursue your passion (or find it if you don't already know it) and that you'll set aside time every day to be with the ones you love.

That's the secret to happiness. Any questions?

Takeaway: Happiness is not something you can possess or reach. Happiness occurs through action by doing what you love or by spending time with people you care about. The key to happiness is finding what you're passionate about because it's something you'd be willing to do for free simply because you enjoy doing it.

THE LASER

By Gerald Fisher

Professor Arthur Schalow was the co-inventor of the laser, which would be something special to put on any resume. The question of legacy has always been very interesting to me. If somebody asked you, "What do you think you will be remembered for?" what would you say? That's a pretty tough question which is why people get very discouraged thinking about that.

Just thinking about this question forces you to think about your life. What have you done that will be memorable? Why will it be memorable? Think of your friends and

(continued)

(continued)

ask how they may have made their mark in the world that will live on long after they're gone.

Ask Arthur Schalow what he thinks would live on after he's gone and he might say, "Charlie and I invented the laser."

One experience that stands out in my mind was when Art and I were both on the Admissions Committee and somebody made a wisecrack, saying that it looks like everybody we're admitting was born between November and February. Of course I replied in my characteristic manner, "That's because people born between November and February are smarter and more gifted." Everybody laughed, that relieved some of the tension, and we went back to work.

At the very next meeting, Art came in with a graph. He had looked up all the Nobel Prize winners since the first Nobel Prize winner in physics, Roentgen, who discovered X-rays in 1901. His graph covered over 100 years of Nobel Prizes with an average of 2.5 per year, so there were in excess of 250 Nobel Prize winners. He had looked up every birthday and plotted the number of Nobel Prize winner birthdays versus month, and found there was no correlation whatsoever. The graph was a horizontal line at best, but the fact that he had even created the graph and researched the facts tells you something about how he thought.

Although Art could certainly have rested on his laurels as the co-inventor of the laser, there was much more to him than that. My daughter attended a school that sent over a young kid to see me who was very smart and needed help building a project. When I asked him what he wanted to do, he told me, "I want to build a laser."

I thought that was a great project so I decided to sign on. However, since lasers weren't my field of specialty, we eventually got bogged down a bit. It wasn't a matter of pride for me whether I helped this student build a successful working laser or not. I just wanted to help get this laser working correctly, so I went to see Art.

I explained to Art that I had a high school student who was very smart and wanted my help in building a laser. I asked Art if maybe he had a graduate student or post-doc with some extra time who could help us out a little.

To my surprise, Art said, "I'll do it."

The idea that the inventor of the laser would volunteer his time to work with a high school student was very generous, very kind, and very special. However, I said, "I don't think it's something we should do. I know you're extremely busy, and I really don't think that would be appropriate."

Art insisted, "I'd be happy to do it. Unless, of course, you prefer someone else?"

I had to tell Art, "I don't prefer someone else. I just think it would be more appropriate to ask someone else."

Art eventually recommended one of his post-docs, who was very much willing to help this high school student, and I was happy to be part of this interaction. Together, they built the laser and the project was a success. Ironically, 20 years later, this post-doc is now a major scientist and head of his lab in laser physics.

(continued)

(continued)

Now there's the question of, why did this post-doc volunteer? Even more intriguing is, why did Art volunteer? Both men apparently agreed to help this high school student because that's just the kind of people they were. They were both warm, sweet, and kind. Not only were they generous with their time, but their actions demonstrated without hesitation that they were truly concerned about other people, and that kind of behavior was contagious with everyone they met.

Art could have been a typical sort by hiding behind his co-invention of the laser and winning a Nobel Prize, but his willingness to help others did not make it more difficult for him to be a success. In fact, his kindness enhanced the productivity and morale of everyone who worked with him so Art's kindness actually helped make him more successful.

CHAPTER 3

Believing in Yourself

Let me tell you a story about a man who didn't know what he wanted. Because he didn't know what he wanted, he drifted aimlessly through life. He never caused any trouble but he never did anything worth remembering, either. Since he didn't know what he wanted, he listened to what other people told him he should do.

His parents knew what had worked for them so they wanted him to follow in their footsteps. That meant following the well-trodden path of going to college, studying hard, and getting a good job after graduation. This path promised security, but it didn't quite hold his interest.

His friends didn't know what they wanted, either, so they were content to take life one day at a time. One day, they promised themselves, they would figure out what they wanted to do but until then, they would just have fun. This path seemed the most appealing, but it did become repetitive and monotonous, like running on a treadmill that ultimately felt like nothing more than a dead end.

Other people he met, guidance counselors, relatives, and acquaintances, all had different ideas what he should do and they all gave the best advice they thought he could use. Like the path laid out by his parents, these many paths offered seemed proven and safe, but they also felt like they weren't just quite right either, like putting on a pair of jeans that was a size too small or too large.

All the messages he got from society told him the same thing. Be happy. Be responsible. Be like everyone else. Such vague messages left him more confused than ever.

What he saw on television, read in the newspapers, and heard on the radio confused him even more. Information was everywhere, but none of it seemed to help. This man had his whole life ahead of him, but he felt he could gather more and more information forever and still never know the right answer.

While he watched others live out their lives, this man felt a growing sense of despair. Everyone seemed to know what they were doing but him.

He wanted to do what they did, but it didn't feel right.

He thought he could do what they said, but it didn't sound right.

That's when an idea suddenly hit him like a bolt of lightning. The only person who could decide what he should do with his life was him.

And that was the hardest decision he had ever made in his life.

That man is me, but it could be anyone. In the last chapter, I explained how you create happiness through action by following your passion and spending time with the people most important to you.

While it's easy to pick out the people you care about the most, whether they're family or friends, it's far more difficult to not only identify your passion, but to summon up the courage to go out and get it.

If your passion happens to follow a clearly defined path, you have it easy. Suppose your passion is to heal people who have been physically hurt through accidents or disease. The path to fulfilling that dream can be as straightforward as going to medical school and graduating so you can start practicing medicine. While the effort needed to get into medical school and become a doctor definitely isn't easy, the well-defined path to becoming a doctor is as simple to follow as connecting the dots in a coloring book.

Unfortunately for many people, pursuing their passion won't lead them down well-trodden paths to completion. Instead, they have to blaze their own trail.

So not only will most people need to go where few have gone before, but they'll need to summon the courage to risk venturing into the great unknown while everyone around them tells them it can't be done.

That means trusting yourself that you know the direction you're heading and believe it will eventually take you there no matter how long it takes. That's never easy to do, especially when everyone around you tells you you're wrong and that you're heading for disaster.

Remember, nothing worthwhile will ever be easy. If it was easy, then everybody would be doing it.

History is often made by people whose names we do not know – like the 1,300 steel workers who worked around the clock to make the *USS Yorktown*, damaged at the battle of the Coral Sea, good enough to sail for Midway. They said it would take three months to make her whole again, but Admiral Nimitz said, "You have 48 hours."

As the *USS Yorktown* sailed into Pearl Harbor, steelworkers began making spot repairs – cutting a beam here, welding structural steel there. They worked for 48 hours straight until the *USS Yorktown* had to sail for Midway to catch up with the *USS Enterprise* and *USS Hornet*.

Because of those unnamed steelworkers, the United States had a third aircraft carrier, and that made all the difference. Japan lost the Battle of Midway as their three aircraft carriers were set on fire in six minutes (and ultimately, Japan lost four aircraft carriers, not to mention the planes and skilled pilots that went with them). The *USS Yorktown* was sunk at Midway but not before she gave a terrific account of herself.

The next time you're tempted to do what's easy, remember the story of the *USS Yorktown*. Then you'll realize that the path to success often goes through the hardest road possible.

EASY IS THE ENEMY OF SUCCESS

When Steve Wozniak and Steve Jobs created one of the first personal computers in the world, they proudly showed their invention to Steve Wozniak's boss at Hewlett-Packard. Yet Hewlett-Packard wound up turning Steve Wozniak down five times. The company simply couldn't understand how a primitive personal computer could possibly be a successful product.

The easy path would have been to give up. Rather than get discouraged, the two Steves decided to start their own company and call it the Apple Computer Company. To raise money, Steve Jobs sold his VW van while Steve Wozniak sold his Hewlett-Packard scientific calculator. After building and selling the Apple I computer, the pair finally hit commercial success with the Apple II computer.

With neither business experience nor the benefit of familiar procedures to success, Steve Wozniak and Steve Jobs had to learn as they went along while adapting to the fast-growing and ever-changing personal computer market.

Now that Apple is a trillion-dollar company with popular and influential products like the iPhone, iPad, and Apple Watch, it's hard to believe that the company teetered on the brink of bankruptcy multiple times. When faced with failure, doubt, and unknown, unfamiliar situations, it would have been easy to give up and choose a safer, more established path such as getting a job with a company like Hewlett-Packard again.

What kept the two men going wasn't intelligence, hope, or fear. It was their passion.

Steve Wozniak loved the engineering challenge of designing personal computers long before there was even a market for personal computers. Steve Jobs loved the idea of creating technology that could enhance human potential. Getting ordinary jobs would never have satisfied their passions. As a result, their passions gave them the persistence and determination to succeed.

Even if they had failed, Jobs had told Wozniak that they could at least tell their grandchildren that they had once started and owned a company of their own. That idea was the difference between giving up and continuing to pursue their dreams.

Remember, money is irrelevant. Even though Apple eventually made both men wealthy, they were never motivated by the money but by their own passion. Success isn't about money or power but about changing your life. When you change your life, you often change the lives of those around you.

Daniel Kish isn't a household name. Neither is he a billionaire entrepreneur like Steve Jobs and Steve Wozniak. What makes Daniel Kish unique is that he took a major challenge – inability to see – and discovered a passion that would help not only himself but others find freedom in mobility.

After losing his sight as a baby when he was diagnosed with retinal cancer, Daniel learned about echolocation, which is how bats navigate in the dark by emitting squeaking noises and hearing the echoes to avoid obstacles around them.

Daniel Kish also uses echolocation by making clicking sounds with his tongue that helps him create a mental image of his surroundings from the reflected noise. This has allowed Daniel to walk and even ride a bicycle through an obstacle course without hitting a single object.

Daniel has now taught several hundred blind children around the world how to use echolocation to increase their mobility and independence. Daniel may not be a household name or a multi-millionaire, but by developing echolocation as a way to navigate the world without the aid of a guide dog or a cane, he has helped other blind people gain their freedom.

Nobody taught Daniel how to use echolocation. Yet Daniel did the "impossible," but he isn't alone. Thomas Tajo, a boy born in a Himalayan village, became blind at an early age. With no training, he also taught himself how to use echolocation. He now researches the evolutionary history of the senses and presents his findings at scientific conferences all over the world. Ben Underwood lost his sight at age three. By age five, he too taught himself echolocation to the point where he could play basketball, rollerblade, and skateboard as well as a sighted person.

You always have a choice. You can do what's easy or you can do what's hard. Doing what's easy often means following clearly defined paths that others provide for you. If your father is a lawyer, it might seem easy to just go into law school and become a lawyer at your dad's firm. Instead of taking this seemingly easy route, Bill Gates decided to drop out of school and create Microsoft.

If you come from a poor family with no education and you're a black woman, it might be easy to feel like you don't have a chance and not even try. Yet that didn't stop Oprah Winfrey from getting her own talk show on a black radio station. When she proved popular as a radio talk show host, she hosted her own television show and later created her own network. Today, Oprah is a billionaire, but her success is less about money and more about her determination. She avoided the easy way out and did the hard work of using her speaking skills to help and inspire others. She didn't do the hard work to get to a distant goal she had no guarantee of ever reaching. She did the hard work because that's the type of work she enjoyed doing whether she got rich from it or not.

Any time you're faced with a choice, look for what's easiest and look at what's hardest. Chances are good the easy way will involve less struggle, less pain, and less resistance. That's what makes the easy choice seem most appealing. But that's exactly why the easy way can often be the absolute wrong choice.

Keep in mind that the easy way doesn't necessarily mean it's easy to achieve. The easy way just requires no conscious decision or risk from you. Going to medical school and becoming a doctor is definitely not easy, but it can be a much easier choice than telling your parents you want to drop out of college so you can make a living playing the guitar.

The easy way often leads to a hard life later.

The hard way often leads to an easy life later.

The easy way often offers a clearly defined path, and that's what makes it so tempting because there's less risk and uncertainty. However, if the easy way is not what you truly want, it will always be the wrong path for you, even if it might be the right path for someone else. One major key to happiness is to never try living someone else's dream and that's often what the easy way is all about.

Besides a clearly defined path toward success, the easy way may also promise the twin temptations of money and security. After all, who wouldn't want money and who wouldn't want the security of a well-paying job?

Once again, money and security may make you feel secure, but they won't make you happy. When you do something just for money, you're basically a prostitute. When you avoid risk in exchange for security, you might as well live in prison.

The easy way offers safety, certainty, money, and security. That's what makes it so appealing to everyone around you, including your friends, relatives, and parents. When you play it safe, you won't risk getting hurt physically, emotionally, or financially. When you gravitate toward certainty, life becomes more predictable. When you strive for money, you'll be able to enjoy the finer things in life. When you cling to security, you hope your life will never experience any unexpected and unwanted surprises.

But playing it safe and embracing certainty means you'll never experience the emotional highs and lows that come from achieving any type of success. Rather than riding a roller coaster with intense turns and breathtaking drops, you'll be riding a stationary horse on a carousel that's slowly spinning around and going nowhere. When you value money and security over your own dreams and curiosity, you'll often wind up with cash that feels little more useful than play money, and when you embrace security, you'll often find that it's another word for monotony and boredom.

The easy way may be tempting, but the ultimate price will cost you control of your own destiny. There's always a price to pay in any choice you make. If you choose the easy way, the price will be high in the end. If you choose the hard way, the price will be high in the beginning and could continue being high all the way to the end.

There are no guarantees in life. When you look for a guarantee, you're ultimately chasing an illusion.

In the movie *The Matrix*, human beings have two choices:

1. Wake up and spend every moment struggling for their own freedom.

2. Close their eyes and spend the rest of their lives dreaming as a lobotomized human vegetable.

Guess which option guarantees safety, certainty, money, and security? Now guess which option most people choose and discover only too late that they made the wrong decision in the end?

Fear motivates far too many people. In their quest to avoid failure, people often sacrifice what makes them special, and that leads to a life drained of emotion, energy, and happiness.

MAKING CHOICES

The only difference between the easy way and the hard way is what you want to do. At every moment in life, you'll have major choices that can drastically change your life. When you're young, the choice may be what to do out of high school. Do you go to college, and if so, which college, and what will you study? If you go into the military, which branch will you go into, and what do you want to specialize in? If you want to start a business or pursue an entertainment career, what's the first step to get started and how will you support yourself?

When you get older, another life-altering choice may be to stay in your current job or switch careers. Do you want to get married to the person you're currently dating or stay single? If you do get married, do you want children right away or do you want to wait?

Any choice can be the right one for you, but you should never choose what seems easiest, even if the task itself is actually extremely difficult (such as going to law school or starting your own company).

When faced with a major decision in your life, list as many options as possible. Then go through each option and ask yourself why this option is appealing to you (not to someone else, such as your parents or your spouse). If an option doesn't strike an emotional chord in your heart, chances are good it's not the right option for you, no matter how attractive it may seem to others.

Go through this list by yourself until you get rid of everything you know you don't want. The end result will be one or more options you do like. In many cases, you may not like or want any of your options at all.

The biggest problem with choice is that you often need to make a decision without feeling you have enough information to choose wisely. The problem is that if you wait until you get enough information to choose wisely, the time to make that decision may be gone. Every choice involves uncertainty.

More importantly, you absolutely must embrace your passion. If you don't know what you want out of life, everything and anything can seem appealing. Without passion to act as your guiding star, you'll risk making choices because you're friends are doing it, because it's available where you live, because it appears easy, because it looks lucrative, because it seems like what you should do, because your parents or peers are pressuring you to do it, because it's the latest trend, or a million other reasons, none of which connect to your true passion.

The best choice for you will always be the one that brings you one step closer to fulfilling your passion, regardless of what anyone else might think.

If any of your options promise to bring you closer to your passion, that's likely the right choice for you. If none of your options feel like they can help you achieve your passion, your best option is to look for what might be your first step.

Even if one of your options may seem to bring you closer to your passion, stop and ask yourself, are you choosing this option because it's available or because it truly is the best option available? In many cases, the best option is to look for what might really be your best option.

Back in high school, Sam Raimi knew he wanted to direct movies after his dad brought home an early film camera. So Sam started making movies in high school with his friends.

After graduation, he had a big decision to make. The obvious choice was to go to school and study filmmaking. Yet Sam took the harder route, dropped out of college, and raised money from investors so he could make his own movies. After making several films, he created *The Evil Dead*, which became a cult hit and launched his career.

Would he have been as successful if he had taken the seemingly safer and obvious route of studying filmmaking in college? We'll never know, but we do know that by taking a chance and pursuing his passion, Sam Raimi achieved his dream of making movies for a living, where he's now an accomplished Hollywood director who directed the first *Spider-Man* movies starring Tobey Maguire.

YOU ARE YOUR OWN WORST ENEMY

No matter what choices you face, absolutely no one can ever stop you. Other people can make your life more difficult, but in the end, only you can decide whether you'll let other people stop you. Some people may actively get in your way, others might strongly discourage you, and still others might even threaten you. That's why taking a stand and choosing your own life is the hardest decision in the world.

But here's the secret. After you do it once, it will get easier to do a second time, and then a third. However, it works the other way, too. If you let others make major life decisions for you, it gets progressively harder to keep saying no to others and keep saying yes to your own ideas until you allow the opinions of others to smother your dreams for good.

We all have only one life to live. Everyone gets the same 24 hours each morning, so it's crucial that you spend your time the way you want. Your life is ultimately your own, and you must embrace your decisions however they may turn out.

It all boils down to taking responsibility – and that's what people fear the most.

If you let others choose your life for you, it's easy to blame anyone but yourself if it all goes wrong. However, if you choose your own life and it goes wrong, you have no one else to blame but yourself.

That's scary, but that's the harsh truth.

Here's another secret. Even if your choice winds up going horribly wrong, you always have the power to make another choice to turn your life around.

When you go through life letting others decide for you, you risk always feeling helpless no matter what happens.

When you go through life making your own choices, for better or worse, you'll slowly develop the courage and trust in yourself to make different choices as your life goes on. That can't help but build your character and make you emotionally and psychologically stronger so you can gradually create the life you want to live.

But the first step is to get out of your own way. Your biggest enemy is always yourself.

LEARN TO TRUST YOURSELF

Everyone can hear voices in their head. Usually they're the voices of your parents, your spouse, your friends, and yourself. Most of the time, those voices will try to discourage you from doing anything. You'll hear phrases like:

- "Who do you think you are?"
- "It's never been done before."
- "You don't know what you're doing."
- "You're not smart enough."
- "It will never work."

- "You need to know your place in life."
- "That's too risky."
- "What if you fail?"
- "What will other people think?"
- "Nobody can do that."
- "You don't have enough _____ (money, education, connections, etc.)."

It's always easy to come up with a million reasons why you shouldn't make a decision by yourself and why you should listen to experts, friends, parents, and relatives instead of your own heart. Since these negative voices will never stop, use them. Every time you hear another negative thought come in your head, realize that these negative voices are really trying to protect you.

Then go ahead and make a decision anyway.

When faced with a life-altering decision, people tend to freeze and not know which option is the "right" one. The truth is that any decision is the right one because there is no single "right" answer.

Would your life have been better if you had made a different choice? You'll never know. Would your life had been worse if you had made a different choice? You'll never know. No matter what you choose, you'll never know if you chose the best option.

Guess what? It doesn't matter.

The second you make a decision, you've started training yourself that you have the courage to trust yourself. Just as you can strengthen any muscle through exercise, so you can also strengthen your own self-worth and belief in yourself through constantly taking responsibility for your own decisions. The more you trust yourself, the stronger you'll grow as a person.

On the other hand, the less you trust yourself, the more dependent you'll get on others, and the further your life spirals out of your control. Eventually you'll feel you have no control over your life and that's the worse feeling in the world.

So start trusting yourself by making decisions and taking responsibility for them. The more decisions you make, the more you'll trust yourself and the easier it will be to decide for yourself.

By taking responsibility and making your own decisions, you'll truly mature and grow up. The only way you can lose is if you do nothing at all.

THE "BUT I DON'T KNOW ENOUGH" EXCUSE

Most people don't do what they want. One reason is because far too many people don't even know what they want out of life. A second reason is that people may know what they want, but don't know the first step they should take.

If you don't know what to do first, then you automatically know what you need to do first. Namely, your first step is to figure out what that first step should be.

Many people don't know what to do so they do nothing at all. Here's the truth. Any time you want to do something new, you're always going to be a beginner and not know everything you should do. No matter how smart you may be or how much education you may have, you're never going to have all the experience necessary to do something new without making plenty of mistakes.

When faced with the unknown, far too many people prefer to wait until they know more. Unfortunately, by doing nothing, you'll never know more. At some point, you must believe you can learn as you go. Waiting to know what you're doing first means you'll never try anything at all.

The first time Babe Ruth stepped up to the plate, he didn't know if he could hit a home run. Michael Phelps has won the most Olympic medals in history (28), but the first time he competed, he didn't know if he was good enough to win even one Olympic medal. At one time, everyone starts out as a beginner. The only way beginners can ever become experts is by throwing themselves out in the world and learning as they go along.

That means plunging ahead without knowing everything. When you don't know everything, you can't help but make mistakes. The key is knowing that each time you learn from a mistake, you become more knowledgeable and confident. Then one day, you'll find yourself completely confident of your abilities.

Confidence doesn't come from knowing everything ahead of time but by knowing that no matter what happens, you have the skill, intelligence, persistence, and determination to keep moving forward anyway.

Unless you never do anything at all, you'll always be venturing into unknown territory. You may never know enough but it doesn't matter. What does matter is that you believe you'll always be capable of learning anything as you go along.

The next time you're afraid that you don't know enough, you're probably right. So make your next step to figure out what you need to learn to keep moving forward anyway.

DREAM ABOUT THINGS YOU'VE NEVER IMAGINED POSSIBLE

In *Alice in Wonderland,* Alice tells the Queen, "One can't believe impossible things." To which the Queen responds, "I daresay you haven't had much practice. When I was your age, I always did it for half an hour a day. Why, sometimes I've believed as many as six impossible things before breakfast."

This passage from Lewis Carroll's classic book might seem nonsensical, but there's a serious message inside. The fact is that no matter who you are, you can't help but be shaped and influenced by the world around you. Whether you're rich or poor, your environment molds your thoughts on what you believe is possible.

Grow up in a wealthy environment and you might think nothing about raising funds to start your own company. Grow up in a poor environment and you might think the pinnacle of success is having your own apartment. A poor person might never imagine starting an international business, while a rich person might never imagine that anyone on the planet could die from dehydration due to a lack of clean water. If you only make choices based on what you see as possible, there's a good chance you'll miss other options that you didn't even know existed.

Whenever you're confronted by a choice, it's easy to come up with options. However, you can't choose the best option if you don't think it's even possible. Therefore, play a game with yourself. Any time you're faced with a choice, list the first options that come to mind. Those choices will come from your particular background.

Then imagine the options a completely different person might have when faced with that same choice. What options would a poor person see? What options would a rich person see? What options would someone of the opposite sex see? What options would someone from another country see?

By forcing yourself to think outside your normal parameters, you can expand your options of what's possible. The greater the number of choices, the more likely you'll find the best choice for you.

So practice imagining the impossible. You may surprise yourself at the opportunities you suddenly see that were right in front of you all this time.

MAKE A DENT IN THE UNIVERSE

Steve Jobs, the co-founder of Apple, once said, "We're here to put a dent in the universe. Otherwise, why else even be here?"

When you identify your passion, you've made a huge step in defining your purpose in life. When you trust yourself enough to make choices to help you fulfill your passion, you're well on your way to a satisfying and fulfilling life.

Despite embracing your passion and consciously making a choice to pursue it, a tiny nagging doubt might pop up in your head from time to time.

"Am I doing enough?"

The answer is always yes. Your passion doesn't have to change the world. It doesn't have to save the planet. It doesn't even have to make a lot of money.

All your passion has to do is make you happy, and that's enough to change your world. Happiness is contagious. It's impossible for a mad, angry, or sad person to make another person happy, but it's easy for a happy person to help another person find happiness.

Once you start following your passion, you'll change your own life.

Once you change your own life, you can inspire others to change their lives.

Once others change their lives, they can help change the rest of the world.

When Jobs urged people to "make a dent in the universe," he didn't mean that everyone had to start a trillion-dollar company like Apple. You can make a dent in the universe by making your child smile today. You can make a dent in the universe by giving a total stranger a sincere compliment. You can make a dent in the universe by picking up a piece of trash off the sidewalk. You can make a dent in the universe by saving the life of an animal. You can make a dent in the universe by just being the real you.

Once you start a daily habit of "making a dent in the universe," you'll suddenly notice the tremendous power you do wield, however small it may seem. You don't start by changing the world. You start by changing yourself, and once you change yourself, you'll start changing the world without even realizing it.

The real you is hidden inside. By following your passion, you can coax it to come out, little by little. By taking small steps to bring you closer to fulfilling your passion every day, you make it easier for the real you to slowly emerge and eventually blossom.

The real you is your passion. The more you nurture your passion, the more you nurture your true self. The biggest dent in the universe you can ever make is learning to trust yourself.

Takeaway: Only you can live your life. You will never have all the information you need to navigate through life, but you must trust that you'll be strong enough to get through, no matter what happens. You can only choose those options you know about, so it's in your best interest to expand your list of options so you can choose the best option at all times.

NOBEL LAUREATE ROBERT HOFSTADTER

By Gerald Fisher

Robert Hofstadter is often described as the nicest, kindest person anyone ever met. In fact, he was one of the reasons I came to this graduate school and in my tenure, I found this assessment to be 100 percent true. We went to the same undergraduate college, City College, in New York.

He was the reigning Nobel laureate, meaning he had received the Nobel Prize the year that I was making my application. So I accepted the university offer, drove across country, and my first stop was at the university physics department parking lot. I looked on the ledger in the main lobby, identified his office, marched down the hallway, and knocked on his door.

I introduced myself and said, "I'm a new graduate student and I'm also from City College." Isn't it great to be 20 years old and stupid? He invited me in and spent an hour with me.

He took out a map of the campus and circled the campus pool with a big heavy marker that almost went through the paper. He said, "We have a great swimming complex here, which includes a great pool. You have to go down and get a locker." I said I would definitely do that.

We were chatting for more than an hour, and finally I realized that I had taken more than enough time from Professor Hofstadter. I got up and thanked him, saying that I couldn't imagine a better introduction to the department. He said, "It was wonderful; come anytime. I loved hearing about City College, and I would love to hear about the wonderful work that you're going to do."

So I wobbled to the door and limply put my hand on the doorknob. I opened it and he said, "One other thing. You can do me a favor." I said anything that I can do, and he said, "Please call me Bob."

Calling the reigning Nobel laureate, one of the greatest physicists in the world, by his first name did not work for me. There are just some things you just don't do. You don't

(*continued*)

(continued)

call Albert Einstein "Al." You don't call Mozart "Wolfie." This first act of kindness was matched by all of our interactions, and there were many, many over the years. But I have to admit that it took me four or five years before I could call Professor Robert Hofstadter, Bob.

Only once did my father ask me what I actually did. I took that opportunity and tried to explain about research and studying the laws of nature and how and why things work the way they do, and so on. He listened politely. When I finished, there was a long silence. He stared at me, collected his thoughts, and asked, "And they pay you for this?"

Only once did he come out to California to visit me. We were walking around the physics department and Bob Hofstadter came out of his office. I introduced my father to Professor Hofstadter. Bob told my father that he also grew up in the Bronx and went to Clinton High School. My father said, "Oh, I went to Theodore Roosevelt High School." They really seemed to be getting along which, by the way, was another marvelous attribute of Professor Hofstadter.

The next thing I knew, one of the greatest physicists of the twentieth century took my father into his office and spent an hour talking to him. My dad asked him, "What actually does my son do?" Bob tried to explain in much the same way as I did and with as much success. My father particularly wanted to know what he should say to his brothers when they asked, "What does Jerry do?"

Finally Bob just said, "Tell your friends and your brothers that he's a teacher."

Bob Hofstadter won his Nobel Prize the year that President Kennedy had his reception in the White House for all the Nobel laureates. Because Bob Hofstadter was the reigning Nobel Laureate for that year, he and his wife Nancy had a private dinner with John and Jacqueline Kennedy, the president and first lady of the United States.

I said, "Wow, that must've been really special."

And Bob said, "Well, it went okay until my tie went into the soup, and I was very embarrassed." Nancy responded, "There was really no surprise there, because your tie always went into the soup."

Bob's kind and generous nature infused his research group and infused me. I knew that I could always go into Bob's office and just chat. He loved to do that and I loved to talk to him about his past.

One time I was to introduce him, which wasn't a big deal since I had done it many times before. As I progressed through the resume document, I saw something that stunned me, so much so that I must have paused for over a minute. At lunch, Bob asked me what happened, saying that the pause was so long and so obvious that he thought I had taken ill.

I said I hadn't noticed it before, but you were at Princeton in the 1940s, which means that you were there with Einstein."

He just said, "Yeah."

"Yeah?" I said. "That's your reply? I've known you for over 20 years and you never mentioned it? Maybe you never saw him – or when you did, he was aloof and distant?"

(continued)

(*continued*)

"Not at all," Bob replied. I saw him every morning when I came into the department. He was genial and friendly and even greeted me by name. He was always warm and personable.

"So what was the problem?" I asked.

Bob said, "The problem was every time I tried to approach him, I would choke up. He would say, 'Good morning Bob,' and I would reply, 'Arggwpd.'"

I'll always remember Bob as a sweet, gentle, wonderful man, and always remember how much I owe him.

CHAPTER 4

Choosing Your Own Path

Hollywood loves zombie movies and TV shows. Zombies are the reanimated corpses that stagger about in search of human flesh to consume. Zombies are often called the "walking dead" because even though they can walk just like a regular person, they're brain-dead inside, so their movements are purely mechanical.

While zombie movies and TV shows may be scary, there's an even more frightening type of zombie that you can see around you every day. These type of zombies may not eat human flesh nor are they reanimated bodies of people who have already died. The zombies I'm talking about are people who are the true walking dead.

These real zombies are people who never take a chance, never make a stand, never make a choice, and ultimately, never really live. You may have seen these people before. In the words of Henry David Thoreau, "The mass of men lead lives of quiet desperation."

That's because far too many people wait for life to come to them rather than actively going out and grabbing the life they want to lead for themselves. When you passively wait for life to come to you, you'll probably be waiting a lifetime.

Everyone knows of the man who could have made a fortune if only they had made the right choice. Everyone knows of the woman who could have been a success if she had only kept going. Everyone knows somebody full of talent, loaded with skills, and blessed with good luck, who still wound up living a life of mediocrity.

The biggest tragedy isn't that people are starving, lacking health care, or suffering from poverty. The biggest tragedy is when someone fails to realize all the wonderful gifts they truly possess and yet refuse to believe they even have them. Without ever finding their passion and embracing their principles, these people are the true horrors of the world.

Fortunately once you identify your passion and define your principles, you won't have to live a life of quiet desperation. That's because passion helps you decide what you want to do. Then your principles help you define how you're going to *take action:*

- Action can get you started.

- Action can keep you moving a little bit closer toward your goal every day.

- Action can get you back on track when obstacles and interruptions get in your way.

- Action is the only way you'll ever reach any dream. You'll never achieve anything worthwhile by just wishing for it. You can only achieve anything worthwhile by getting out of your comfort zone and taking a chance that you could fail.

The secret to success is paved with failure, and the only way you can overcome failure is to keep taking action to make your life better a little bit at a time. It may never be easy, but in the long run, it will always be worth it by giving your life purpose and meaning.

FEAR: THE IMAGINARY OBSTACLES

The biggest reason most people never pursue their passion is fear. It's not that they don't have enough money. It's not that they don't have enough education or knowledge. It's not even that they don't know how to get started. People fail because they let fear control their lives.

Actor Robert Pattinson, who appeared in the *Twilight* series, said, "I used to get so paralyzed with anxiety before auditions I just couldn't do anything."

Surprisingly, many A-list actors have experienced stage fright during auditions, performing on stage, or acting in front of the camera. The difference between success and failure is as simple as refusing to let fear stop them from trying anyway. Courage isn't the absence of fear but acknowledging your fears and doing what you want to do because the rewards are far greater than not doing anything at all.

The most common fear is the fear of failure, which can mean anything from fear of embarrassing yourself in front of others, fear of losing all your money, or fear of not knowing what to do. When you fear failure, you might think it's safer not to try at all. Of course if you don't try, you've already failed.

If you're afraid of failing, your fear of failure can hold you back. Rather than boldly strive forward to get what you want, fear of failure can make you hesitate. When you hesitate, you'll risk substituting bold action for timid steps that feel safer to avoid committing yourself completely. While tiny steps are better than no steps at all, at some point in your journey, you're going to have to take a big leap forward, and a timid little step just isn't going to get you there.

Just remember that fear can never hold you back. What's really stopping you is you and your own imagination.

Fear is nothing more than a negative, imaginary outcome. In other words, fear is the belief of what could go wrong, but it is not the certainty that anything could go wrong.

Every time you let fear get in your way, you're really imagining the worst possible outcome and believing it's not only going to come true, but it's much larger and more frightening than it could ever be:

- Maybe you'll go broke. (Can you picture yourself living on the streets with your family and slowly starving to death?)

- Maybe you'll get hurt. (Can you imagine breaking every bone in your body and not being able to get to a hospital?)

- Maybe you'll look foolish. (Can you imagine the whole world laughing at you?)

- Maybe you'll lose respect. (Can you imagine being shunned by everyone around you for the rest of your life?)

- Maybe you'll even die. (Can you imagine the most horrible death possible?)

Not only does fear imagine the absolute worse possible outcome, but fear exaggerates the possible dire consequences of what could possibly go wrong. When you let fear overwhelm you, you're no longer dealing with real problems that you can solve. Instead, you're facing an imaginary monster that can never be killed because it feeds off your thoughts to keep getting bigger and stronger.

When fear runs rampant in your imagination, it's easy to give up on your dreams just to make that fear go away.

If you let that happen, you're letting an imaginary obstacle stop you from accomplishing a real goal. That's no different from being afraid to sleep at night because you think there's a monster hiding in the closet.

Here's how fear works. It scares you once, and if you let it succeed, it grows a little bigger and comes back again. Each time you run away from it, it gets bigger and comes right back at you once more. Ultimately, you have to make a decision. Will you keep endlessly running away from your fear and letting fear control your life? Or will you face your fear and deal with it, no matter what happens?

What's the easy way? Keep running. What's the hard way? Stand up and face your fear knowing that it could defeat you.

But if you keep running away from your fear, it's already defeated you. Given a choice between letting you fears defeat you or taking the chance to confront and overcome your fear, what will you do? The choice boils down to whether you're going to accept certain defeat, or whether you're going to take a chance for possible victory.

Ultimately, you have to ask yourself, am I going to let fear control the rest of my life or am I going to take control of my own life? If you're not willing to let other people control your life, why would you let your own fears do it instead?

GETTING STARTED ANYWAY

Fear will never go away. Even the most experienced Broadway actors and musicians selling out entire stadiums feel fear before the curtain rises. Taylor Swift talks to herself in the mirror to calm herself down before going on stage and repeatedly tells herself that "it's going to be okay." The only difference between fear and courage is that fearful people let their fears stop them, while courageous people feel fear but go ahead and do what they want anyway.

Singer Lorde said that her stage fright can get so severe that she actually gets sick. "I, like, totally threw up before my show last night. I am reduced by nerves. I can be completely crushed by feelings of all kinds . . . I get nervous, I get freaked out, I get, you know, the usual stuff."

Actress Jennifer Lawrence said, "I never feel like, 'I've got this.' I'm always very nervous and aware of how quickly people can hate you and that scares me."

Opera singer Andrew Bocelli said, "Stage fright is my worst problem . . . So there's always this fear, because you feel naked. There's a fear of not reaching up to expectations."

Singer Donny Osmond said, "I know when I walk out there, I'm not going to give the best performance. I'll make a mistake. I'll trip. I'll do something stupid. But it's OK; you pick up and just move on."

If major celebrities who make a living performing in front of audiences still feel fear after so many years of performing, just realize that it's okay if you do, too.

Fear is uncomfortable, but it's a reminder that you're alive.

When you ride a roller coaster, those sharp turns, steep drops, wild loops, and out-of-control speeds may make you scream in terror. But you ride that roller coaster precisely to experience that feeling of fear.

Imagine going to an amusement park and never getting on any roller coasters. At the end of the night when the park shuts down, how do you think you'd feel if you had spent the entire day doing nothing at all? You may not have experienced any fear, but neither did you experience any fun, either.

Just remember that fear is part of life. The more you try to eliminate fear from your life, the more you'll cut yourself off from making your life worth living. The only people who have completely eliminated all uncertainty and fear from their lives are the people buried in a cemetery.

Since you can't completely eliminate fear, what you can do is use fear as motivation. If your fears tell you that you might get hurt, move forward anyway but take extra care to protect yourself from physical harm.

If your fears tell you that you might go broke, move forward anyway but create plans for protecting your money. Once you acknowledge your fears and immediately address them, you minimize that fear so it can't paralyze you into inaction.

Remember, if you're not feeling fear, you're probably not doing anything worthwhile in the first place.

DEALING WITH OBSTACLES

No matter what you decide to do with your life, you're going to run into obstacles. The simplest type of obstacles are physical. For example, if you want to pursue a career in country music, you'll probably need to move to Nashville, Tennessee. If you want to pursue a career as a surfer, you can't do that in Iowa or North Dakota. Instead, you'll need to move where the waves are such as California, Hawaii, or Australia.

Physical obstacles challenge you to break out of your comfort zone and do something different. That could be as simple as starting a new habit such as learning how to paint or sing, or it can be much bigger such as forcing you to move to a new location where you don't know anybody in an unfamiliar city.

Doing something new is always scary, because any time you do something new, you'll likely make mistakes. Think of when you learned to ride a bicycle. At first, you probably feared you would fall. As you learned to control the bike, you started getting more confident, and that confidence most likely led you to see what you could do, which likely led to more mistakes.

You can't learn anything new without making mistakes. If we really feared making mistakes, we'd all still be crawling around on all fours for fear of falling if we ever tried to stand up.

The biggest challenge from physical obstacles isn't just the problems they create, but the changes that they force to overcome that problem. It might take time and money, but anyone can overcome physical obstacles such as moving to New York or Los Angeles to break into show business. The hard part is actually doing it.

Physical obstacles force you to change your life by changing your habits, but they are actually the easiest obstacles to overcome. If you want to move to Hollywood to break into acting, it's fairly straightforward to pack your bags and move to Los Angeles.

The second, and far more challenging, type of obstacles, are those created by other people, most of whom sincerely have your best interests at heart. Obstacles created by others challenge your own trust in yourself. When a parent, friend, or relative tells you that your dream is unrealistic, you may get a little defensive. But what happens if several people tell you the same thing? What if absolutely no one you know believes in you or your dream?

You can't just raise a little more money to overcome this obstacle. There's a huge emotional and psychological barrier blocking your way. When people around you try to discourage you from your dream, it's only natural to doubt whether your dream is worth pursuing at all.

Stop. First, ask yourself why someone might be trying to discourage you. In many cases, people have their own agendas. They might want you to pursue their dreams instead of your own. Once you understand someone's agenda for trying to discourage you, it makes it much easier to overcome their objections.

Second, people might want to "protect" you by steering you away from something risky toward something that appears more achievable and safer. There's no guaranteed path to becoming a singer or an entrepreneur, but there is a much clearer path to becoming an accountant or taking over the family business.

When people want you to choose something safer and more predictable, they're really asking you to choose a life that they think is best for you, not what you think is best for you.

Although these people might truly care about you and wish to protect you from getting hurt, following their advice risks choosing a life you don't really want and that will never make you happy. It might make you comfortable, but it will never emotionally satisfy your soul.

Ask yourself: Would you rather risk being free and getting hurt, or hiding in a cage to guarantee you'll never get hurt but that you'll never be happy either?

Perhaps the scariest obstacles from other people come from those who truly love you but are afraid of change themselves. Are you willing to pursue your dream at the risk of leaving someone behind? Are you willing to chase your passion, knowing that if you fail, someone you love will suffer from your failure as well? It's hard enough to risk your own life, but it's twice as hard to ask someone you love to risk their own life with yours.

Keep in mind that if people truly love you, they'll understand your desire. If they refuse to understand, you have to decide what's worth more: your relationship with that person or your passion?

You can have your dream and keep your relationships with your loved ones intact, but if someone refuses to acknowledge your dream and refuses to help you find a way to achieve your dream, you need to ask if that person truly cares and loves you after all.

A person without a dream risks being nothing more than an empty shell. If you sacrifice your dream for another person, your dream may still burn within your heart. Will that create resentment? Anger? Sadness? Depression?

You need to decide what's more important, your dream or your relationship. It may not be an easy decision, but only you know the answer. Once you find that answer, embrace that decision with all your heart and move on with your life wherever it may take you.

Remember, physical obstacles force you to change the way you live. People obstacles force you to confront your relationships with others. Yet the greatest obstacle you'll ever face will come from your own doubt.

Everyone doubts themselves, even celebrities, billionaire entrepreneurs, and top athletes. You may not think you have what it takes, you're not smart enough, you're not good enough, you don't deserve to succeed, you don't have the right look, you're not young (or old) enough, you don't know what you're doing. Your mind can create a million excuses, and that flood of self-doubt can threaten even the strongest will in the world.

Whenever you're facing self-doubt, always remember that whatever self-doubt you might have, there's no way of knowing whether you have a particular weakness unless you test it. If you just assume you're not good enough, then you'll act like you're not good enough, and that ends in a self-fulfilling prophecy. Self-doubt can only strangle your dreams if you give it that power.

However, if you fear you might not be good enough, stop and ask yourself, is that really true? Banish the false self-doubts that might be nagging you. Don't let a lie sabotage your dreams.

Remember, there are always two sides to every self-doubt. If you think you're not good enough at something, look for ways to get better. If you think you're not old (or young) enough, you can always find a place where you do fit in. Don't dwell on the negatives. Once you examine your self-doubts, you'll find that they can prod you into taking action that can increase your chances of success in the long run.

CHANGING YOUR MIND

There's a famous short story by Frank R. Stockton called "The Lady or the Tiger?" In this story, a man is given a choice between opening one of two doors. Behind one door is a lady whom he must marry. Behind the second door is a ferocious tiger that will kill him.

To help this man decide which door to open, he looks in the stands at his lover, a princess who knows which door holds the lady and which door holds the tiger. This princess points to the door on the right – but there's a problem.

The princess hates the lady behind the door and can't bear the thought of her lover marrying this other woman. However, the princess also loves the man forced to choose between two doors, so will she want to see him mauled to death by a man-eating tiger?

This story shows that making decisions is never easy, because you never know if you're making the right choice. To avoid this, many people would rather avoid making any decision at all, but procrastination simply means wasting time – and who knows how much time any of us have left in our lives?

In "The Lady or the Tiger?" story, the man must make a choice. He can only make one choice. If he makes the wrong choice, he'll die. Fortunately, most choices you'll face will never be this final. Instead, any time you make a choice, you can always change your mind afterward.

If you suddenly decide to move to Los Angeles to break into show business but find you don't like it, guess what? You can always change your mind and do something else. Maybe you still like acting, but prefer to go into theater instead, pursue acting as a hobby, or get involved in a different aspect of acting such as working as an agent or as a promoter to other actors.

If you go to college to become a doctor but decide you aren't that interested in medical school after all, you can always choose something else. Maybe you'd rather be a paramedic, a nurse, a dentist, or some other career related to the medical field. If your passion is true, you just need to find the right way to pursue it.

Steven Spielberg dreamed about becoming a director so he applied to the University of Southern California's film school, but was turned down. Undaunted, Spielberg went to California State University to study film instead.

However, he got an unpaid intern job at Universal Studios, and while working at Universal Studios, he got the chance to make a short film that impressed the studio executives. That's when Universal Studios awarded Spielberg a seven-year directing contract. Needless to say, he decided to drop out of college.

If you've truly found your passion, you'll never want to give it up. However, you may follow one path only to find that choice isn't working for you. Rather then give up on your passion, give up on your current path and look for a new one to continue pursuing your dream.

If you give up on your dream, you were never passionate about it in the first place. If you've found your passion, you'll never give it up, but you may change your mind on how you'll try to satisfy your passion.

There is no single "right" way to fulfill your passion. The only right way is the way that ultimately gets you where you want to go, and that path will be different for everybody.

STAY FOCUSED

When you know your passion and have found a path to help you fulfill it, the next step is focus. Focus means keeping your eye on your desired goal. That means stripping away anything that may distract and slow you down from pursuing your dream.

Time is crucial for achieving any goal, so the more time you spend pursuing your dream, the faster your progress will be. Five steps can help you stay focused:

1. *Schedule time for your own well-being.* You can't succeed in any goal if you're sick or exhausted. Even though billionaire Richard Branson runs multiple companies, he makes exercise a daily priority because he values his fitness and health. Dustin Moskovitz, co-founder of Facebook, said he regretted not exercising and eating better because he would have achieved success even faster without the health problems he had to overcome.

2. *Schedule time for your loved ones.* Billionaire Sheryl Sandberg said that she makes sure to leave work at 5:30 every night so she can be home, because her children are her priority. Founder and former CEO of Intel, Andy Grove, would also consistently leave work at 6:30 each night, regardless of any problems within the company, because he wanted to be home for dinner.

3. *Schedule time to pursue your dream.* Apple's CEO Tim Cook regularly wakes up at 3:45 a.m., while former Disney CEO, Bob Iger, woke up at 4:30 a.m. By getting up so early, you can have large blocks of uninterrupted time to think, return email messages, exercise, and plan your day. If you don't schedule time every day to move one step closer to your dream, it's far too easy to let daily activities interfere and distract you until there's no time left at all.

4. *Eliminate anything that interferes with your first three priorities: your health, your family, and your dream.* You want all your daily activities to move you in the

same direction. If you exercise every morning but
spend your lunch eating junk food, you're working
against yourself and slowing down your own progress.

5. *Avoid multitasking.* Trying to do two or more things
   at once might seem efficient, but when you do two
   things at once, you likely won't do either task very
   well. A Stanford University study found that when
   people multitask, they're more easily distracted and
   have a harder time transitioning between tasks than
   people who focus on one task at a time. Multitasking
   creates the illusion of efficiency but actually gives you
   nothing but the reality of performing two or more
   tasks poorly. If a task is worth doing, it's worth doing
   well. If a task isn't worth doing well, it's probably not
   worth doing at all.

   Famous martial artist and movie star Bruce Lee
said, "The successful warrior is the average man, with
laser-like focus." That means anyone can succeed in
anything they choose to do, just as long as they remain
committed to achieving their goal.

Your daily schedule gives you the freedom to take control over your life. You just need to set aside the time to do it
right now.

REMEMBER YOUR PASSION

If you think creating and maintaining a schedule feels too cum-
bersome and time-consuming, think of it as simply a tool to help
you get what you want. If you wanted to travel from Los Angeles
to Berlin, it might be a hassle to get through airport security and
cram yourself in an airplane, but you do it because it's the fastest
way to get to where you want to go.

Likewise, you create routines and define schedules because it's the fastest way to get you where your passion is taking you. You likely need to do many unpleasant or annoying tasks to achieve your dream, but in the end, it will all be worth it.

Your passion is the driving force that can help you overcome doubt and fear so you'll even get started. When people feel the energy behind your drive, they'll be attracted by your passion and that attraction can put you in touch with people who can help you toward your dream.

David Lucatch, founder and CEO of Yappn Corporation, a real-time translation service, said, "The people I have seen achieve the greatest success in their professional and personal lives are passionate people that lead, support, and mentor others with that 'zeal and zest' for the work and people."

Dr. Dre, the rapper who co-founded Beats, a company that was acquired by Apple, had this to say about talent in music and business, "You can learn it. But in order to be good at it, to be really great at it, it has to be in you."

Passion not only gives your life direction, but also helps act as a guide to make sure you stay on track. The minute you stray from your passion, you know you're making a mistake and need to change course to get back on track in a way that aligns with your passion. Howard Schultz, CEO of Starbucks, said "If we compromise who we are to achieve higher profits, what have we achieved?"

When problems inevitably arise, passion will give you the energy to keep going no matter how great the setbacks may be. Without passion, you have nothing. With passion, you have everything.

Never forget your passion. It's what literally drives your life forward.

TAKE A LEAP OF FAITH

At some point in your life, you're going to be faced with a decision that only you can make. What's worse is that you'll need to make this life-altering decision using incomplete information with no guarantees for the outcome. What will you do?

That's when you need to carefully examine your choices and look at which option speaks to your heart. Then close your eyes, take a deep breath, and go for it regardless of the consequences or hardships ahead of you.

That's scary. That's unpredictable, but it's also liberating because letting go of your fears means you may be putting faith in yourself for the first time in your life. Just remember, no matter what you do, it likely will never be the end of the world. If you make a choice for all the right reasons, it may not turn out the way you want or expect, but it will give you tremendous confidence in yourself, and that's the greatest feeling in the world.

What happens if you never trust yourself and always play it safe? You'll likely go through life always wondering what could have been. Then each time another life-altering decision appears, you'll risk shying away from it until you never make any important decisions at all.

Watch any great movie and you'll notice a common factor. The hero always controls his or her own fate. Regardless of what obstacles get in the way, heroes find a way to overcome and emerge victorious, but that first step always involves taking a giant leap of faith into an unknown world.

Be the hero in your own life. At some point, life will force you to make a decision. Play it safe or take a chance. What will you do? What would your favorite movie hero do?

One final word of advice. Don't compare yourself to others. This is not a race or a competition. If someone else achieves a goal like yours, that doesn't mean you can't get there, too. Life is not a zero-sum game where someone must lose in order for someone else to win.

In life, everyone can win. If you're going to compare yourself to anyone, compare yourself to your old self from the past. This will let you measure who you are now and who you were a day, a week, a month, or a year ago. By making steady progress, you can see how much further you've come compared to your past self in another time.

When you compare yourself to others, it's easy to get depressed or feel envy or jealousy. When you compare yourself to yourself, it's much easier to feel happy about what you have accomplished. Focus your energy on becoming a better version of yourself. As noted writer Oscar Wilde said, "Be yourself; everyone else is already taken."

Ultimately, the secret to happiness lies in taking action to pursue your passion, spending time with the people you love, and focusing on the present because that's the only moment any of us ever have, and the present is the only place where you can experience happiness.

No matter what you do with your life, you'll always have to find your own way because no one has ever faced the exact same circumstances as you. As American poet Muriel Strode (August 1903 edition of The Open Court periodical) said, "I will not follow where the path may lead, but I will go where there is no path, and I will leave a trail."

Takeaway: The only way to get what you want is to take action. Emotional obstacles can be much more difficult to overcome than physical obstacles because you often need to overcome your own doubts. Schedule time to pursue your dream and be sure to practice gratitude to remind yourself of your successes every day. No matter what you do, you'll need to find your own way to success.

The Two Presidents

By Gerald Fisher

I knew two presidents of the university. The first I only met once but that was super memorable for me and I suspect also for him. The second was one of those experiences that not only lasts a lifetime but actually helps to shape one's perspective and destiny.

The first one had to do with my research in nuclear physics. You may have seen people who work in a nuclear area wearing radiation badges that show if you've been exposed to any dangerous radiation. I had been working in the nuclear group for about five or six years when I precipitated this event.

The way these badges work is that you wear them while working and place them back on the rack when you leave the lab. Once a month, the badges are collected and shipped for evaluation. The business of reading radiation exposure is hardly a big business, so the whole operation was handled by one fellow who did the work during the graveyard shift of one of the local private companies. The interesting thing is that when the reports were completed and returned each month, everyone's radiation exposure read zero. Month after month, every member of the group for all these half dozen years was recorded with radiation exposure of zero. Nobody got exposed to anything.

So my curiosity got the better of me. I took the hottest, most active source of radiation we used for experimental purposes and put it right on top of my badge and left it there for 24 hours.

Then I forgot all about it. The badges were duly picked up and transported to the company where the fellow was going to check them. What he does is take the film out of the badge, dip it in a solution, and look at it. Darkened areas mean there has been an exposure to radiation and lighter areas mean no exposure.

So he went through these badges, saw only clear films, and wrote down all those zeros. Then he picked mine up and saw that it was jet black. That meant the person has received a massive dosage of radiation and he's probably lying somewhere in the corner, and might even be dead.

He had been doing this sort of work for quite awhile and knew the procedure well. For this serious an occurrence, he called up the president of the university at 4 o'clock in the morning, who called up the dean of arts and sciences, who called up the chair of the Physics Department, who called up the head of our group.

I have to admit that the head of our group delivered a profound comment about me, which I guess has to be regarded as an insult.

He stopped the person recording this issue in mid-sentence and asked, "Is this person with the horrendously large exposure perhaps Fisher?"

The department head probably thought that my advisor already knew something about Fisher and this large exposure to radiation, so he quickly replied, "Yes, it is!"

My advisor then said, "Well, let's just forget it for this evening. There's probably some dopey explanation."

(continued)

(*continued*)

The next morning he called me into his office and told me my little prank had caught the attention of everybody on campus and that I had a 10 o'clock appointment with the president. That's how I got to meet the president.

I had to go see him at 10 o'clock that morning to explain myself. I walked in and he was sitting there. I sat in the guest chair and he was there yawning.

I explained what I did and he said, "That's ridiculous, but don't let it happen again."

Some years later my advisor confessed, saying, "You know that prank with the radiation badges? It was a silly thing to do but I often wondered about all those zeroes too, and I'm glad, sort of, that you did what you did."

The second presidential experience was so positive that it has lingered in my memory for a lifetime. I was doing freshman advising at the time when one of my freshman came in and she was distraught. It was 1980, and her father, a member of the foreign service, was being held captive in Iran. I knew of this, so my immediate thought was that something had happened to him.

She then showed me a letter. It said how proud we at this university are to have a student on campus whose father is serving his country in such an admirable way. It then added, however, that unless the full tuition for the spring quarter was in hand by 8 a.m. Monday morning, she would not be allowed to register.

I found this hard to believe and then promptly lost it completely.

I told her to wait and headed out for the quad and walked down the corridor until I reached the president's office. I entered and the secretary said, "Sir, you can't go in there."

I said, "Yes I can." It probably is no surprise that the president has multiple secretaries and assorted personnel working in the office complex. I walked by all of them. They didn't know me. I could have been a lunatic with a gun.

I was lucky, I guess, and made it to the door of the president's private office. His head assistant said to me, "Sir, you cannot go in. The president is having a very important meeting."

I walked into his office anyway, and there was indeed some sort of meeting going on. The president said, "You are interrupting an important meeting and I must insist that you leave."

I said, "This is more important that anything you might be doing."

He looked puzzled. Later I found out that he had hit his private button to summon the police.

When we were alone and before the police arrived, I showed him the letter that my student had received.

He mumbled, "Holy _____ !"

Then he picked up his phone and said, "Put Fred on the phone."

Fred's secretary said, "Mr. President, he's in a meeting."

(*continued*)

(*continued*)

"Then get him out of whatever that meeting is. This is very important."

Fred got on the phone, the president read the letter, but Fred and the registrar claimed to know nothing about it.

The president then said, "I am not calling to level blame. I don't care about that now. You are to meet with this young student on Monday morning and you are to see to it that she registers in every one of her chosen classes. There will be no closed classes, no waiting lists, no nothing. She is to be inserted wherever she wishes and, if there are any questions, you are to say that this order comes directly from the president."

I said to the president, "I am just falling over with gratitude. If there is anything I can ever do for you . . ." He just smiled.

I asked him to write a short note that I could show the student, and he complied. Speaking of smiles, I cannot describe the look on her face when I showed her the note.

That was probably the nicest, but stupidest thing that I had ever done. Now if we just had more people like this university president, the whole country would be much better off, just by demonstrating kindness and generosity to help someone else.

CHAPTER 5

Hazards Along the Path to Passion

There's a reason why pilots go through checklists before taking off. A checklist forces them to examine everything about an airplane from the engines and flaps to the fuel gauge and lights. Checklists ensure that pilots don't overlook something that could cause huge problems once they're airborne.

Even though pilots may have thousands of hours flying airplanes, they go through checklists before takeoff every time because they know it's far too easy to forget one thing, and that one thing could spell the difference between success and failure.

Before you set off pursuing your dreams, you also need to go through a similar checklist. Your personal checklist needs to verify what you're doing and why you want to do it. That way you'll be able to avoid problems much later.

LIFE IS SHORT

Visit any cemetery and you can see plenty of people who no longer have a chance to pursue their dreams. Life is far shorter than you might realize. When you're young, it's easy to think life is long. When you get older, you realize how short life really can be.

If you were to die in the next five seconds, what would you regret not doing?

List everything you would regret not having done.

Now go out and do it.

George Lucas originally wanted to become a race car driver. While practicing his racing skills one night, his car got broadsided and flipped over. For three days, he lay in the hospital, hovering between life and death. When he finally regained consciousness, he began a spiritual quest to find out what his purpose in life was. This spiritual quest led him to read a large amount of science fiction, which helped steer him toward filmmaking and ultimately create *Star Wars*.

Until you realize how short and precious life can be, it's easy to feel like you have all the time in the world. Once you realize you could die with your dreams still locked inside of you, that will give you the motivation to start pursuing your dreams right now.

Watch your favorite movies and look for a common storytelling technique known as a "ticking time bomb." That's where the hero has to achieve a certain goal by a specific time or the villain will win. Because the hero can't wait, he or she must take action now or all will be lost.

You are the hero in your own movie; knowing you have a limited time on Earth means you cannot afford to wait on your dreams. You must take action now. Your life literally depends on it.

INERTIA IS EASY, CHANGE IS HARD

Any time you're unhappy with your current state in life, stop and ask yourself what you would rather be doing instead. In other words, take back control and responsibility for your life. That means you may need to take a chance by changing or leaving your current way of life.

That's the hardest decision anyone can make.

That's because it's easy to keep doing what you've always done, even if it doesn't excite or inspire you any more. Inertia is easy. Change is hard. Doing something different is always hard. Doing the same thing you've always done is always easy.

But easy is also the enemy of growth because if you just keep doing what's easy, you never challenge yourself. Without forcing yourself to learn and adapt, life risks becoming nothing but a colorless existence. As an infant, it would have been far easier to keep crawling on all fours rather than take the trouble to learn how to walk. Yet we all learned to walk because we chose to do what wasn't easy at the time.

Every morning, remind yourself that it's your life and take responsibility for where you're at. Once you realize you got where you are through your own efforts (or lack of effort), you can then decide what to do next.

In many cases, people don't want to take control of their lives because they fear making a mistake, not making the right choice, or even upsetting someone close to them for not living up to their dreams. So they let someone else choose for them because it's easier than picking their own options.

Of course by letting others decide your life, you've indirectly chosen your life anyway. Whether you like it or not, you've always been in charge of your life. The only difference is whether you want to acknowledge it or not.

The moment you're ready to take control of your life, you've done something many people never do their entire lives. Being in control of your life can be scary since you may not feel like you know what you're doing precisely because you probably don't know what you're doing. But you have to take responsibility for your life anyway. If you don't control your life, other people will do it for you and you most likely won't like the choices they make for you.

So your choices are to take responsibility for your life and take a chance, or give up responsibility and let someone else tell you what you should do.

Whether you deliberately choose your life or whether you let others shape your life for you, you're making a decision. One choice lets you actively create a life pursuing what makes you happy. The other choice lets you hope that others will create a fulfilling life for you even though nobody but you knows what happiness means to you. Given these options, you can see that taking charge of your life really is the only option after all.

TRUST YOURSELF

Nobody knows everything, and that includes you. That means when everyone's bombarding you with criticism and even the world seems to turn against you, there may be nobody who believes in you. That can be the loneliest feeling in the world.

Whenever you feel the deepest pit of despair, remember, you were not put on this Earth for nothing. You must trust that your life has a purpose because you can give it a purpose.

Everyone might think you're crazy and everyone might think you're wrong, so how do you know if they might be right and you might really be crazy and wrong?

The answer is simple.

Ask yourself, "If I achieve my dream, will it force me to improve myself and give me the opportunity to help others?"

When dreams force you to improve yourself, you must take time to develop new skills. If you do not enjoy the effort needed to develop specific skills, that's a huge warning that you're probably chasing the wrong dream. The sooner you can recognize this, the sooner you can find the right dream for you.

A second criteria is that a dream should be bigger than just you. Goals for selfish purposes are often small. Goals for selfless purposes are often much larger.

One way to expand your world is to volunteer for a cause you believe in. Not only will this force you into a new, exciting, unfamiliar world, but it will put you in contact with many amazing and inspiring people you may never have met otherwise. When I decided to volunteer at my daughter's school, I learned so much about the problems and challenges of teaching and education that I never knew before. I met so many sincere and dedicated teachers and administrators who face the daily challenges of guiding our youth to becoming stronger, smarter, and more confident in their abilities.

When you help others solving problems much bigger than yourself, you realize how many intelligent and caring people there are in the world who share your values. That alone can make you feel a little less lonely in the world and a little more powerful in what you can do together. More importantly, you also learn how you can contribute to any solution, regardless of how much or how little you may believe your skills may offer. When you're part of solving important problems much larger than yourself, you realize just how much you can contribute to making this world a better place for everyone.

Ricardo Semler didn't take over the Brazilian company Semco Partners just for the power or money but because he wanted to prove to the world that you could run a profitable business based on industrial democracy where all the workers had a say in the company's direction.

The first day as CEO, Ricardo fired 60 percent of all the top managers because he felt corporations could thrive best when all employees felt empowered to do their jobs, free from the autocratic hierarchy found in most corporations. Even back in the

1980s, Ricardo was one of the early advocates for establishing a healthy work-life balance for all employees, not just for upper management. Ricardo didn't want to just run a profitable company; he wanted to run a successful company that made every employee feel valued and important.

Elon Musk didn't start his Boring Company just to make money, but to overcome the problem of traffic congestion in cities. He didn't start Tesla just to make electric cars but to help drive the world away from fossil-fueled vehicles. He didn't start SpaceX just to launch rockets but to reduce space exploration costs to enable further exploration of the solar system.

In other words, dreams that can help others may not be so crazy after all.

As long as you're enjoying the journey to whatever goal you're seeking, you're already a success, no matter what material rewards (or lack of them) you may have.

Don't worry about what's practical, realistic, or attainable. Think what you want to do without limitations. At one time, nobody had heard of a drone operator, a podcast host, a ride sharing driver, a professional esports gamer, a social media influencer, or a mobile app developer. Yet all those career options popped up because of changes in technology. Who knows what new career paths tomorrow might bring? Just because something doesn't exist today doesn't mean it won't be available in the near future.

Trust yourself. For many people, that can be the hardest decision in the world.

PASSION + PURPOSE = DIRECTION

Far too many people never find their passion. Without passion to energize their lives, people often drift through life, never living a bad life but never living a memorable and joyful life either.

Rather than enjoy the highs and lows of life, they prefer to cower within the shadow and safety of blandness and mediocrity.

When you avoid risk and excitement for safety and certainty, you have no direction. Only when you combine passion with purpose can you find a direction for your life. So that means you need to define your purpose.

That purpose can be anything you wish, whether it's to raise a happy, loving family or start your own company that can clean up plastic waste from the world's oceans. Your purpose is not just what has meaning for you, but also what can help others. The more your purpose can help others, the stronger it will be. You can focus on helping as many people as possible (quantity) or just focus on helping a much smaller number of people close to you (quality). If you fail to help others with your purpose, your overall impact can't help but be much smaller if it's only for your benefit. That might make you happy momentarily, but it's also a narrow, limited view of life when you can create so much more.

When you just have passion, you'll have a lot of energy but with nowhere to use it. When you just have a purpose, it will be too easy to get discouraged when faced with obstacles because you'll lack passion to keep you going no matter what gets in your way. However, when you combine passion and purpose, now you have a direction.

- Passion identifies what you want to do.
- Purpose funnels your passion toward a specific goal.

The combination of passion + purpose gives your life meaning because now you not only know what you want to do, but you know where you want to go. Just knowing that puts you ahead of 90 percent of the world that either does not know their passion or does not know their purpose. As a result, they do not know where they want to go in life.

If your life feels like it's going nowhere, it's probably because you don't have a passion combined with a purpose. It's easy to set goals, but it's much harder to stay committed to them unless you truly care about them. You may be passionate about something, but you don't know how to express it until you combine it with a purpose. Only until you have passion with purpose will you feel your life has meaning.

DEALING WITH COMPETITION

No matter what you pursue, you will have competition. The best way to deal with competition is to ignore it and focus solely on what you can control, which is you. If you can consistently improve your skills, you'll separate yourself from your competition anyway.

In nearly every field, there's plenty of room for everyone. Although there can only be one NBA champion team each year, there's always room for superstars to excel on any team. While only one person can win an Oscar for Best Actor each year, that doesn't mean other actors can't perform to their utmost ability. The real rewards don't come from outside recognition but from knowing you did your best.

In the business world, you cannot ignore competition or you risk going out of business. In any field where there are rewards, you'll always find competition. Rather than fear competition, find a way to overcome it.

Amazon has put scores of companies out of business. At one time, electronics retailer Best Buy was in danger of getting wiped out by Amazon. Rather than compete against Amazon's strengths, Best Buy chose to capitalize on its own strengths while eliminating Amazon's advantages.

One huge advantage Amazon offers is low prices. When rivals fail to match Amazon's prices, customers simply purchase those identical items from Amazon. In fact, customers would engage in a tactic known as *showrooming*. That meant customers would walk into stores like Best Buy to see and touch a product, then buy it through Amazon at a lower price. Showrooming helped kill major retailers who had the expense of leasing retail space, only to see their customers purchase from Amazon instead.

So Best Buy simply matched Amazon's prices. Now customers could see a product and buy that product right away from Best Buy instead of waiting for it to arrive in the mail from Amazon.

Anything worth pursuing will always attract competition. Since you can never eliminate competition, you must learn to deal with competition by finding ways to make yourself the best option available whether you're an actor, an athlete, or a business.

Once you make yourself so distinct that people can only get what they want from you, you'll never have to worry about competition again. Starbucks, McDonald's, and Walmart have plenty of competitors, but that isn't stopping them from succeeding every year.

As comedian and author Steve Martin said, "Be so good they can't ignore you." Your competition can't control how good you get. Your talent is totally under your control. Even though Sammy Davis Jr. faced racism and discrimination, he still excelled in show business because he became so good the world couldn't ignore him.

Ultimately, the only competition you ever have to worry about is anything that threatens to keep you from devoting time and effort to improving yourself.

YOUR DEFENSIBLE ADVANTAGE

Once you have an idea of where you want to go, it's tempting to rush right out to pursue it. However, stop and think first. Rushing will likely create mistakes that you could have easily avoided if you had just taken the moment to think and plan ahead.

Just as you wouldn't rush to catch the first plane out of the airport that might not take you where you want to go, you shouldn't rush to pursue the first opportunity you think will help you get to your goal.

No matter what your goal might be, start where you are. Most people have what I call a *defensible advantage*. That means they have something in their life that can give them some kind of benefit or advantage that other people may not have. For example, many college students feel lost with no direction. Despite this feeling, their defensible advantage is their opportunity to take the time in college to examine alternative fields of study, spend time volunteering in different organizations to see what they may like, and meet different people from fellow students to professors. In most cases, students can do this without the nagging worry of paying a mortgage, supporting a family, or dealing with major health or family issues.

Another defensible advantage most people have is where they live. No matter where you live, you're likely surrounded by family and friends who can help you in some way. It's far easier to get help from someone you know than from a complete stranger.

Starting from your hometown can also help you see for yourself if you're committed to your goal. There's no shame in pursuing something, only to find out later that you don't like it as much as you may have thought. Then you can just start the process all over again in finding a new direction for your life.

Where you currently live may not offer all the opportunities you want, but it can likely give you a safe place to start. For example, suppose you want to be a musician. You could pack up and move to Nashville or New York to hit it big. If you're just getting started as a musician, this would mean competing against more established and experienced musicians in an unfamiliar city where you must find a place to live, find a way to make money to pay your bills, and find time to get better as a musician. This essentially triples the number of obstacles in your way.

On the other hand, if you just stay where you are, you likely have a place to live and a way to pay your bills. Now you can just focus on becoming better as a musician. This approach removes a tremendous amount of stress from your life and gives you time to get better at your craft. Eventually when you outgrow your current location, you can then consider moving to another city. Keep in mind that you can always come back to your home town again if things don't work out in a different part of the world.

Perhaps you're currently stuck in a job that you don't like. Rather than quit and suddenly have to worry about paying your bills, your job (however distasteful it may be) provides you with financial stability so you can afford to take classes in other fields to see what you might like without worrying about where your next meal may come from.

No matter who you are, chances are good you have some kind of defensible advantage that you can fall back on if the worst should happen. Use this defensible advantage as your fallback position. It may not be where you want to stay, but it can give you a stable base so you'll have one less thing to worry about as you pursue your dreams.

Making a decision and changing your life can be scary, but as long as you know what your defensible advantage might be and how you can return to it if necessary, you'll have that safety net, knowing that the worst that can happen is you'll just wind up back where you started. Then you can always try again.

Your defensible advantage acts like a stepping stone to help you get where you really want to go. Some people may have more advantages than others, but you have to start with what you have and build from there. Remember, every house must have a solid foundation to build on so look for your defensible advantage and use it to help you get to where you want to go in life.

PLAYING IT SAFE

Many people are afraid of failure and making a mistake so they want to play it safe. Instead of reaching for their dreams, they settle for what they know they can achieve. Rather than strive for greatness, they prefer the security of what they already have. The idea of playing it safe can be the most limiting and destructive thought in the world because it stops you before you can even get started.

Playing it safe might seem like a practical strategy until you realize it's based on avoiding mistakes. The best way to avoid mistakes is to avoid doing anything different, and the only way you can do that is by continuing to do whatever you're already doing right now. That means whatever you're doing now in your life is the only thing you'll be doing decades later.

If you're fine with that, then there's no reason to change. However, if the idea of spending the rest of your life doing exactly the same thing for the rest of your life sounds less than exciting, you need to realize the first rule about playing it safe.

Imagine you only have one day left to live. Looking back on your life, would you have any regrets for what you wish you had done? If not, then you're probably living a happy life. However if you would experience any form of regret if you didn't do something, then you know you absolutely must pursue that goal to make your life feel complete.

Playing it safe isn't about avoiding mistakes. It's about planning ahead, knowing you're going to make mistakes anyway. Mistakes are inevitable whether you're trying something new or simply repeating the same actions you've done for the past 30 years. The only sure way to avoid mistakes is to do nothing at all. The moment you try to do anything, you open yourself up to making a mistake.

When people go through life trying to avoid mistakes, they're essentially trying to protect themselves. Nobody likes making mistakes, but you can't learn anything without making mistakes. How many mistakes did you make learning to stand on two feet when you were a baby, or how many times did you fall down while trying to learn to ride a bike as a child?

Mistakes are part of life. Unfortunately, far too many people mistakenly believe that mistakes are something to avoid at all costs, which means avoiding risk of any type as well. Given a choice between the risk of making a mistake or the false safety of doing nothing at all, too many people choose to do nothing at all, and that's the biggest mistake they can ever make in their lives.

You don't want to take foolish chances, but you also can't afford to play it safe since playing it safe means taking no chances at all. Risk is part of life. The key is that the more times you risk failure and learn you can survive, the less frightening any type of risk will feel.

If the idea of failure still frightens you, start by taking small risks and gradually build up your tolerance for taking chances. Find a different way to work, the market, or your home. Try eating in a different restaurant or order a meal that you wouldn't ordinarily pick. Listen to different radio stations or watch different TV shows. Use your less-dominant hand to brush your teeth or control the mouse or trackpad on your computer. Get into the habit of taking small chances, and you'll eventually feel comfortable knowing you can take larger chances.

Fear is never going to go away. People aren't brave because they have no fear. People are brave because they charge ahead regardless of how much fear they really do feel. Most people let fear paralyze them in their tracks because they imagine what could go wrong. Yet in many cases, these imagined disasters will never come true at all, which means if you let them stop you, you're letting something that doesn't exist keep you from pursuing your dream.

Mark Twain even said, "I am an old man and have known a great many troubles, but most of them have never happened."

If you wish, play it safe by taking the safest path to your goal. As long as you're pursuing a goal you want to reach, you may just surprise yourself at how much you can change your life faster than you might have thought possible.

NEVER GIVE UP

In the face of hardship, doubt, and fear, it's easy to give up and look for easier options. No matter what goal you pursue, you will encounter obstacles and disappointment. Each obstacle that gets in your way gives you a new choice. Do you continue pursuing your dream or do you choose something else?

There's no shame in changing your mind. There is shame in changing your mind simply because you're looking for an easier option that won't involve much work. Anything you choose will involve work. The trick is finding a dream so compelling that no obstacle will stop you from doing it. That's where your passion comes in to keep you going when times may look tough.

While we would all love to pursue a dream with no problems whatsoever, that's not realistic. Every goal involves obstacles you'll have to overcome. As long as you're passionate about your goal, you'll have the energy to overcome any obstacles, no matter how large or frightening it may be. If avoiding obstacles ever seems like the more appealing option than pursuing a dream, that's a big clue that you don't have enough passion to pursue that dream. That's when it's time to find another goal that you can and will be passionate about.

Never abandon your dreams, because that means you literally abandon the meaning and purpose of your life. Actor Kevin Costner, the star of *Dancing With Wolves*, said, "I think one of the first things to go as people's lives start to go down is their dreams. Dreams should be the last thing to go—dreams are the things you go down *with*. If you're left clinging to a piece of driftwood in the middle of the ocean, I'd put on it the word *dreams*."

Just remember that no matter how many obstacles may get in your way, you'll never know how close you are to reaching success. Think of every obstacle as getting you one step closer to your goal because you never know which obstacle will be the last one in your way. If you give up now, you'll never know how close you came to success. Many of life's failures are people who did not realize how close they were to success when they gave up. This is presented as a statement of 1877, as quoted in *From Telegraph to Light Bulb with Thomas Edison* (2007) by Deborath Hedstrom, page 22.

Jack Canfield and his co-author Mark Victor Hansen created a book idea that they pitched to over 130 different publishers, who told them no. Finally they managed to get a small publisher in Florida to say yes to their idea and that book turned out to be the *Chicken Soup for the Soul* series that has gone on to sell over 500 million copies worldwide.

What did 130 publishers not see in this phenomenal bestseller? We'll never know, but the fact that this book became a massive success was due to the persistence of Canfield and Hansen, who never gave up on their dream despite getting rejected so many times. When you get rejected once, it stings. When you get rejected over a hundred times, you may start doubting yourself. Don't.

Nobody knows everything, even the so-called experts in their field. As long as you can see a clear benefit for others if you should succeed, then that can be further motivation to keep going, knowing how much you can help others in the end. If your dream only involves helping yourself, then it's far easier to give up when you receive a handful of rejection.

You may not have heard of Jack Ma, but he's the richest man in Asia and runs one of the largest companies called Alibaba. Despite his massive success in starting Alibaba, Ma applied for over 30 different jobs (including working at KFC) but got rejected. He also applied to attend Harvard 10 different times and got rejected each time as well.

Despite facing so much rejection in his life, Jack Ma went on to create one of the largest companies in the world. After he proved so successful, he was even invited to give a commencement speech at Harvard, the school that had rejected him 10 times.

Rejection is inevitable any time you take a chance. The only way you can avoid rejection is to avoid taking any risks, and by avoiding any type of risk, you also avoid pursuing anything beyond what you already have. Change of any kind involves risk – and risk always involves rejection. The way to overcome rejection is a strong belief in your idea and a passionate desire to do the activity despite any rejection you may face.

So make sure your dream can benefit others and that you're truly passionate about your dream. If you truly enjoy the activity needed to pursue your dream, then you've already won. Remember, success is more than just reaching your goal but enjoying the journey on the way as well.

Boxing champion Muhammad Ali said, "Don't quit. Suffer now and live the rest of your life a champion." Basketball star LeBron James said, "I like criticism. It makes you strong."

Whatever obstacles may be in your way, you can overcome them. The only thing ever stopping you is you.

Takeaways: Only you can live your life, so only you can choose what's best for you. Goals give direction and can be as big or small as you wish. The right goals for you involve your passion. Passion gives your life meaning. Happiness is created, not found. You can create happiness every time you follow your passion or strengthen your relationship with those you care about most.

TWO FAMOUS PEOPLE

By Gerald Fisher

I want to talk about two people that I didn't know, but meeting them in and of itself were very special occasions for me. One was Jonas Salk, who everybody knows as the inventor of the polio vaccine.

Now as I said before, it's pretty incredible to have as your legacy that you were the inventor of the laser. Most of us can't look back in that manner, but Arthur Schawlow could say that about his legacy.

But if you think about it, Jonas Salk's contribution at least equals and probably exceeds that of Art Schawlow. In fact there is probably no greater legacy in the universe than to have invented the polio vaccine.

The polio vaccine came to us in the 1950s when I was a young teen, so I don't know the horror of polio in the 1920s and 1930s. There were polio victims in iron lungs. Even Franklin D. Roosevelt, the president of the United States, got polio and was crippled for life.

One time, Dr. Jonas Salk was invited to campus. They kept it very quiet. It wasn't in the newspaper, it wasn't in

(continued)

(*continued*)

the campus paper, and there was no announcement. There were only a select few people who were invited to meet with the inventor of the polio vaccine. But of course, word got out, and there were 7,000 people there.

Well, I had to meet him; I had to shake Jonas Salk's hand. He was sitting down because it's pretty hard to meet 7,000 people, and at any given time there were 500 people waiting in line to meet him. I pushed my way into the line and very loudly said how sorry I was. "I know this is rude, but I have something I have to say to Professor Salk."

So I got in line, and a few moments later was standing not two feet away from the great man. I extended my hand. He shook my hand and I said, "There's something I've always wanted to say to you."

He looked up at me with an expression that said he had heard it all, and said, "Yes, what is it?"

I looked him straight in the eye, made sure we had eye contact, paused for dramatic effect, and said, "*You* are going to heaven."

I got him. I could tell that I had gotten to him That's what I wanted to do.

He paused for a second, and then the expression on his face changed entirely, and then he nodded his head and said, "Thank you. Thank you very much."

I was just overjoyed. If anyone in the history of the human race deserves to have someone tell him that he is going to heaven, it was Jonas Salk, the man who eradicated polio.

The other person who everyone knew, I met while working in the physics department on a Sunday. I was dressed even sloppier than I would be normally during the week. I hadn't shaved, my hair was all over the place, and I was wearing shorts and sandals.

I got hungry, so I came out of my office and went down to the main area to see what I could scrounge and there were a hundred people there. I saw all the secretaries and staff there and I knew they wouldn't come in on a Sunday unless it was something special – and of course, it was graduation day.

The university conducts its graduation with everyone in the big theater in the big stadium, and then each department breaks off for its own ceremony. The physics department was arranging itself in the grassy area outside of the main office and I went over and got a little sandwich, which I wasn't supposed to do since I wasn't part of the ceremony.

I was standing off by myself when I spotted a fellow who I recognized but I couldn't place at all. One of the secretaries came over and asked me, "Did you know Mark?"

I said, "Who's Mark?"

She said, "You're staring right at him. He's one of the graduates."

I said, "I was looking at the other fellow in his group. Maybe his father. He looks very familiar to me."

She said, "I don't know his father but I know Mark Armstrong very well."

(continued)

(*continued*)

I was stunned. Armstrong, Armstrong!!! Holy Moly. That was Neil Armstrong, the first man to walk on the moon, and that was his son, a physics major, who was graduating.

The problem was, I shouldn't go over. First of all, it was the graduate's day and I would just be intruding. Second, I looked like something that the dog dragged in, but I just had to do it. The first human being to walk on the Earth's moon. I stealthily made my way and found myself standing alongside Neil Armstrong whereupon I extended my hand. I said how sorry I was to intrude but I just had to shake his hand. Neil Armstrong just smiled and we shook hands.

I managed to say, "Were you really the first human being to walk on the moon?" Brilliant right? Actually I was lucky to get any words out.

And he said, "Well somebody had to."

One of the other professors came over to see what the commotion was and I introduced them. Then this professor asked Neil Armstrong, "And what do *you* do?"

Shaking hands with Neil Armstrong was a great moment for me. Being the first man to walk on the moon may not be an achievement compared to the polio vaccine. It's not an achievement compared to the invention of the laser, either, but it's still a tremendous accomplishment, and it was a tremendous moment for me.

If you ever doubt yourself, just meet someone in person who accomplished something amazing, and that sense of excitement and awe can't help but rub off on you.

CHAPTER 6

Understanding True Success

Once upon a time there was a king named Midas who lived in luxury in a great castle and owned a huge fortune. Best of all, Midas shared his life of abundance with his beautiful daughter. Despite being rich, Midas thought that his greatest happiness came from his gold. He would spend his days counting his golden coins because he believed happiness came from having a lot of money.

One day, Dionyssus, the god of wine and revelry, passed through the kingdom of Midas. One of his companions, a satyr named Silenus, got tired and took a nap near the palace of king Midas. The king invited him to spend a few days at his palace. Dionyssus, grateful to Midas for his kindness, offered Midas a wish as his reward. After thinking about what made him happy, Midas said, "I hope that everything I touch becomes gold." Dionyssus warned the king to think about his wish, but Midas insisted that that was what he wanted. From that day on, everything Midas touched would turn into gold.

Midas touched a table that immediately turned into gold. Then he touched a chair, a door, and a bathtub until he had touched practically everything in his palace and turned it to gold. Seeing so much gold in his palace made him happy. However, when he tried to eat a grape, it turned to gold. Then he tried to eat a piece of bread and drink a glass of water, which both turned to gold.

When Midas's beloved daughter came into the room, Midas rushed to hug her, and turned her into a gold statue.

Now filled with regret and despair, Midas prayed to Dionyssus to take this curse away from him. Dionyssus told Midas to wash his hands in the river and when he did, gold flowed from his hands, but when he returned home, everything he touched turn back to normal again.

Midas hugged his daughter and realized that money was not the source of his happiness after all. Instead, Midas realized that sharing his wealth with his daughter and his people made him much happier. He learned that being generous to others and grateful for what he had was the true source of happiness.

While the King Midas story has been around for centuries, it's a lesson that's still as relevant and powerful as when it was first told in ancient Greece. Money may be fun and enticing because of what it can give you, but ultimately money can never bring you happiness because happiness never depends on wealth or material possessions. Instead, happiness always comes from doing an activity you enjoy and sharing your life with the people most important to you.

Despite this age-old lesson, people mistake wealth for happiness all the time. So before pursuing any goal, ask yourself what success means to you.

For many people, success remains a vague idea that they hope to achieve in the future. Then no matter how much money, power, or fame they get, it's never enough. Rather than define a concrete, measurable goal, people too often set up unrealistic, abstract goals that can never be achieved. This is a sure formula for unhappiness and disappointment because each time you get close to that goal, the goalposts move further away.

True success focuses on what you want to do while spending time with the people you care about. All other forms of "success" are merely distractions. Remember, success is not a possession but an action you take on an ongoing basis.

For example, the story of King Midas shows that money alone can never make you happy. Yet many people continue pursuing money because they falsely believe money will make their lives better. Yet what people really want isn't just more money (or more gold as King Midas found out). What people really want is what they believe money can give them, such as less stress in paying bills, more opportunities to buy things and go places, or freedom from being locked in a job they don't like. Yet if you examine these goals, you'll find that you can still achieve them without a lot of money.

Far too many people have more bills than they can afford. The problem is partially not having enough money, but a more serious problem is that no matter how much money you have, you risk having more expenses than your income. It doesn't matter if you have $1,000 or $1,000,000. If you spend more than you make, you'll always be in debt.

So before you chase the illusion that more money will make you happy, examine your own spending habits. While it's true that unexpected disasters such as medical emergencies or other unforeseen disasters can wreck anyone's budget, most people bury themselves in debt through careless spending. People tend to spend more than they can afford because they're using money as a way to make themselves happy by buying things.

It's always fun to get something new. However, you need to ask yourself if you truly need something or if you're just buying the latest, shiniest new toy to make yourself happy, like a kid opening up birthday presents. There's a huge difference between what you need and what you want.

WHAT POSSESSIONS ARE MOST IMPORTANT TO YOU?

Some people can be happy living in a tiny house that's barely bigger than a truck while other people can live in a million-dollar mansion, own three fancy sports cars, and still be unhappy. It's never how much you own that matters but how much you care about what you own.

Many people love buying the latest electronic gadgets that come out every year, such as smartphones. While buying anything new can give you a brief moment of pleasure, ultimately how much pleasure will that same gadget give you a week from now? A month from now? A year from now? In most cases, the excitement generated by an initial purchase fades quickly, leading you to rush out and buy something else to experience that momentary feeling of pleasure all over again. The end result is a collection of stuff that only clutters your life like a homeless person laboriously pushing an overloaded shopping cart filled with garbage bags containing all of his belongings.

Rather than buy new things, other people spend money treating themselves to pleasant experiences such as dinners in nice restaurants or trips around the world. There's nothing wrong with any of these activities, but if you're only finding happiness by spending money, that's a warning flag that you may be using money to distract yourself because you don't know how to find real happiness in your life.

Spending money is necessary, and there's no need to deny yourself what you enjoy. However, you need to ask yourself what's truly important in your life and what's simply giving you temporary pleasure? By trimming away the objects and activities that cost you money and return only momentary pleasure, you can focus your time and money to buy more of those things and activities that give you far deeper and more lasting enjoyment.

The key is to focus on quality instead of quantity. Less can be more. In many parts of the world that experience floods, wildfires, or hurricanes, people often have to evacuate their homes. If you had to leave your house, what would be your most precious possessions that you would want to pack in the limited space of a car? Chances are good that you wouldn't tow three cars, fill your backseat with a dozen electronic gadgets, or grab a dozen pair of luxury shoes.

Instead, you would likely grab what you couldn't replace. You would take your loved ones, including any pets. You might also grab important documents, such as birth certificates or vaccination records for your child, but that's because they're difficult to replace, not because you especially value them in your own life.

When you imagine evacuating your home at a moment's notice and picturing what you would take, you'll find that most material possessions rank low in importance. That's because you can always buy a new computer or big screen TV. You cannot buy a new child, friend, or spouse, which shows that your relationship with your loved ones is far more important than any objects whether they're a priceless antique or an expensive exercise bicycle.

Look at what's in your life and realize that most of it can always be replaced. Buying replacement items may be expensive but you can always buy a replacement smartphone. However, you can never bring back someone from the dead.

Possessions are fine, but they can never be the true source of happiness. Try evacuating your home one day, and you'll find out how little you may care about all that stuff you may have in every room of your house.

POSSESSIONS OWN YOU

One huge drawback about any material possessions is that they all have a hidden cost that you must pay afterward. At the very least, you'll need a place to store things and paying for that additional storage space can cost money. Some people rent out storage lockers just to keep stuff. Other people clutter their home with more stuff at the sacrifice of having room for other objects they might value even more. When you need extra storage space just to hold all your belongings, chances are good you have too many belongings that are simply costing you in one form or another.

Beyond just storing stuff, many objects require additional maintenance costs as well. Buy two new smartphones when you only need one and now you have the monthly cost of paying for multiple cellular phone bills. Buy two cars when you only need one and now you have to pay to register the car plus pay for additional insurance on each car along with any maintenance costs to keep both cars running.

Owning possessions can require so much time and money that pretty soon you may start feeling like your possessions own you instead of the other way around. When that happens, you can easily feel that you're working for the benefit of your stuff. Eliminate your stuff and you may suddenly find you have more free time and money to spend on something more important.

Owning anything costs money. The less you have, the less you need to worry about storing and protecting it. The more you have, the more you need to worry about storing and protecting all your belongings. Taking care of your possessions can consume a tremendous amount of time and energy. Just look at all the garbage bags homeless people lug around with them wherever they go. They would be much freer with fewer possessions, but like most people, they value their possessions without evaluating what it's really costing them to hold on to them.

The less you own, the less you have to worry about. First, identify the biggest headaches in your life that involve objects, not people. Second, ask yourself if those objects create headaches for you, what benefit do they give in return. Now evaluate whether their benefits are worth the headaches. If not, get rid of those objects.

As Anna C. Brackett said, "We go on multiplying our conveniences only to multiply our cares. We increase our possessions only to the enlargement of our anxieties."

While not everybody needs to renounce material goods, the key is to own your possessions rather than let your possessions own you.

WHAT IS TRUE SUCCESS?

Everyone has an idea of what success means to them and to you. Your parents might want you to do one thing, your spouse may want you to do another, and your friends may want you to do something entirely different.

Ultimately the only measure of success that matters is what you want out of life. It you want to live one way but everyone else wants you to live a different way, you'll never be happy following someone else's measure of success regardless of how much money, fame, or power you might accumulate. If you're not following your own path to success, you can never be a success.

Imagine going to an amusement park like Disneyland and knowing that you can spend an entire day there. Would you want to go on the rides you find most interesting or would you want to go on the rides that someone else tells you they want you to go on? At the end of the day when it's time to leave for home, which choice would have made you happier? If the thought of letting someone else tell you which rides to go on in Disneyland doesn't sound appealing, why would you let someone else tell you how to live your life?

Success has nothing to do with money, fame, or power. Success can take on many forms, but the key is that one person's idea of success may not be your idea of success. To find true success, you must define what that means to you.

When asking yourself what success looks like to you, you have three choices:

1. Look at the options that others present to you.

2. Look at the options around you that others may not promote.

3. Look for options that you may not see around you and that others may not present to you.

Of these three options, the third choice is the hardest but can be the most rewarding.

Let's look at the first and most obvious option, where others give you their version of success, whatever that might be. This version often provides the clearest path to success, such as going to school, getting good grades, and then getting a good job afterward, where you'll magically arrive at success.

As seductive as this path to success might seem, be careful. Just because something is easy and clear doesn't necessarily mean it's right for you. Sometimes when life seems confusing and chaotic, it seems easier to grasp the first path that offers security and predictability. Yet making this type of choice relies more on searching for ease and safety rather than finding out what's right for you. When you sacrifice control of your life in exchange for ease and safety, you're essentially trading the uncertainties of freedom for the certainty of a prison.

While the path to success that others may offer you can be enticing, just realize it's not your only choice. If you decide not to listen to somebody else's idea of success for you, your second option might be to look at the options that you see around you. You might think with so many options, you should be able to find one that you'll like, and you just might.

However, what could also happen is that you'll see only a limited range of choices and choose the best option you like. That's like having a choice between a hundred different foods you don't like and choosing the one you dislike the least. You may have chosen the best option out of all those available, but you also risk still choosing a path to success that doesn't inspire you either.

If you live in a big city like New York or Tokyo, you'll only see those options available in a big city. If you live in a small town in an isolated part of the world like the plains of North Dakota or the desert in Australia, you'll have a different set of options available to you. Yet no matter where you are right now, it's possible that none of the options you can readily see in front of you are ones you want to pursue.

A far better but scarier choice is to decide what you want to do and then go out and do it. This option can be the toughest of all because unlike those options others present to you, finding your own path means you won't have a clear-cut path to reaching your goal.

Instead, you have to blaze your own trail with little or no guidance or help available from those around you. With no straightforward path to success, blazing your own trail to success can be frightening since you don't know if it will even work, how long it will take, or whether you'll ever achieve it at all.

When Mark Zuckerberg started Facebook, social media networks were still in their infancy and nobody knew whether they would ever become popular or just disappear over time like a fad. Anyone trying to start a business based on a social network at that time had no role models to follow. As a result, Zuckerberg had to find his own way to success with no road map or guidance counselors to help him.

Compare the idea of blazing your own trail to pursuing a more straightforward goal like becoming a lawyer. First, you need to get into law school. Then you need to graduate and pass the bar exam. At all times, you know there's an end to your path and you know how far along the path you have to go until you succeed.

Let's look at these three options more closely:

- Follow a path that others want you to choose.
- Pick a path among all available options you see around you.
- Blaze your own trail through an unknown world.

Although there appears to be three options, there's actually only one valid choice and that's to blaze your own trail.

Even if you choose to follow a well-worn path to a goal, eventually that path will end. You may go to school to learn a specific trade or field, but once school ends after you graduate, you'll find yourself out in the world with no curriculum to guide you. Graduate from law school and the school can teach you how to become a lawyer, but they cannot teach you how to find work as a lawyer, nor can they provide guidance for how to work as a lawyer.

When that happens, you'll be on your own. So no matter what choice you pick, you'll have to blaze your own trail sooner or later anyway.

This can be frightening because no one can make your decisions for you. Others can give advice but in the end, you must take responsibility for the decisions in your life and that can be the scariest thing of all.

Ultimately no matter what path you choose, you will have to blaze your own trail because nobody can ever live your life for you. If you're going to blaze your own trail through life, you might as well do it in pursuit of what you truly want.

How to Blaze Your Own Trail

Blazing your own trail in life is the most rewarding option because you literally define the direction of your life, so why don't more people do that? Janice Bryant Howroyd grew up in Tarboro, North Carolina. In 1976, she moved to Los Angeles with just $900. That's when she founded Act I Group, an employment agency. She gradually grew the company until she became the first African American woman to run a company that earns $1 billion in annual revenue.

Steve Jobs attended college for one semester before dropping out. Yet he continued attending classes just to satisfy his own curiosity rather than follow a fixed curriculum. His curiosity led him to attend a calligraphy class where he learned about the beauty of typefaces and fonts. That experience stayed with him after he founded Apple Computers and he used his knowledge of fonts to help create the Macintosh computer.

Notice that both Janice Bryant Howroyd and Steve Jobs could have followed a safe, predictable path that others believed would lead toward success. Yet both decided to find their own path, which resulted in creating two massively successful and profitable companies in the world.

Beyond the financial rewards, both decided to pursue their passion, and that made all the difference in the world. Most people do not blaze their own trail for a variety of reasons that all involve uncertainty, unpredictability, and fear.

Many people go to college because it offers a clear, predictable path. Pass a certain number of classes in specific topics and you'll graduate with a degree. The assumption is that the college degree will help you get a well-paying job. In some cases, that's true. In many other cases, that's dead wrong, which is why so many college students graduate with thousands of dollars in debt and can't find a decent job to pay off their student loans for years.

Even though the "safe" and "predictable" path is anything but safe and predictable, many people still gravitate toward it for another reason. They don't know what they really want out of life, so following a safe and predictable route seems like a better alternative to doing nothing at all.

The problem is that following a safe, predictable route can also distract you from finding your true passion in life. Until you find your passion, no path will ever be the right one. Instead of discovering what you truly love and developing that skill to allow you to make a unique contribution to the world, it seems far easier to follow the safe and predictable route.

As Benjamin Disraeli said, "Most people die with their music still locked up inside them."

Don't be one of those people who live their entire lives and never find their passion. A life without passion is literally no life at all. If you get nothing else from this book, never forget that you are unique. To achieve any type of lasting happiness, you must find what you're passionate about. If you don't know, then spend every waking moment, every day, looking for what sparks your passion. Don't look at what's easiest, what's most profitable, what other people tell you to do, or what everyone else is doing. Look for what speaks to your heart.

Most likely, what you find won't be easy, won't seem profitable, won't be what other people tell you to do, and won't be what everyone else is doing. In the face of so much opposition, it's easy to give up on your passion.

Don't do it.

Henry David Thoreau said, "If a man does not keep pace with his companions, perhaps it is because he hears a different drummer. Let him step to the music which he hears, however measured or far away."

One major reason why people refuse to allow their passion to guide the direction of their life is because of fear. They fear they're not good enough, that there's too much competition, that it's too hard to make a living, that they don't know how to get started, or a million other reasons that seem logical but actually make no sense when you think about it.

If you don't think you're good enough, you probably aren't. That's because any time you're starting something new, you won't know everything you need to know to become an expert right away. Just keep in mind that you can always get better, but the only way you can get better is to spend time learning and practicing your skill until you become better.

Even experts were beginners at one time.

If you're truly passionate about a particular activity, spending time learning and practicing a particular skill won't be a hardship. It will actually be fun. Playing is the best way to learn anything, because you want to spend as much time as possible doing it and you don't mind learning as much as you can to get better. With passion as your motive, learning anything can be fun. Even if you never become wildly successful following your passion, what does it matter when you're enjoying yourself along the way?

Now look at the alternative. Suppose you turn away from your passion because you don't think you can succeed. Instead, you choose another way to live that you're not passionate about, but which can provide a decent life.

How easy will it be to become good at something you don't care about? How easy will it be to succeed when you're competing against others who may be far more passionate about that particular field than you can ever be? Someone passionate can learn much faster and easier than someone who is only mildly interested in a specific activity. That means the passionate person will gradually pull ahead so far that the non-passionate person can never keep up.

More importantly, how will you feel about yourself, knowing you turned away from your passion to embrace a life that doesn't excite you? Given a choice between spending the rest of your life doing something that you love or spending the rest of your life doing something you don't care about, why would you ever think doing something you don't care about would be safer, easier, or more acceptable?

When you turn away from your passion, you're condemning yourself to a lifetime of regret and mediocrity. For the rest of your life, you'll always wonder what could have been if you had only followed your dream. Because you'll always wonder what could have been, you can't help but fail to enjoy the present, which means you'll never be able to enjoy a safe, easy life anyway.

If you choose to pursue something you aren't passionate about, you can't help but live a life lacking in excitement, adventure, and wonder. Try watching a movie or TV show that doesn't interest you. Now imagine watching that same movie or TV show that doesn't inspire or excite you for the rest of your life. How excited would you feel about life, knowing you've chosen to do something that you don't really care about?

Obviously, not everything in life can be fun and exciting, but even the hardest, least agreeable, mundane task can be tolerable if you know it's but a stepping stone to help you follow your passion. However, if you must perform a hard, disagreeable, mundane task that won't get you anywhere closer to your passion, you'll simply be stuck doing a hard, disagreeable, and mundane task for its own sake.

That's a recipe for a lifetime of unhappiness and disappointment. That's why Henry David Thoreau said, "The mass of men lead lives of quiet desperation. What is called resignation is confirmed desperation."

How do you find your passion. Psychologist Mihaly Csik-szentmihalyi created a theory that he called "flow." When people get into a flow in life, they enjoy what they're doing, they can easily concentrate on what they're doing, their actions seem effortless that removes them from the worries and frustrations of everyday life, their sense of self and time seems to disappear where hours can pass and it only feels like minutes.

What puts you in this "flow" is any activity that you truly enjoy and can lose yourself in time and time again. It's that magical feeling where you're truly in the present moment and enjoying every experience.

That's passion.

Not only must you find your passion in life, but you must trust yourself that following your passion is the right decision even if you have no clear path toward success. The truth is that if you're passionate about something, you'll have no trouble spending large amounts of time finding your own trail to success, whatever that might be.

Finding your passion is the first step. Trusting yourself is the second step because once you trust yourself, the idea of venturing into the unknown won't seem as uncertain and frightening any more.

The fear of making a mistake or not knowing what to do can stop most people. But if you're truly passionate about something, making mistakes won't matter because it will keep you involved in what you're most passionate about anyway. Best of all, each mistake will teach you something that will let you continue devoting more time to pursuing your passion.

Musician Taylor Swift tried to break into the music industry by sending demo tapes of herself singing Dolly Parton songs. When this only led to rejection, Swift decided, "I need to figure out a way to be different."

That's when she started writing her own songs and learned to play them on her guitar. Her first success in show business wasn't in the music industry at all but as a model. Although modeling wasn't what she wanted to do, that helped get her the attention she needed to finally break into the music industry, which is what she did want.

Wlad Marhulets left Poland and came to America with just $300. Even worse, he couldn't speak English. Despite this handicap, he kept applying to the prestigious Julliard School to study music. After working on his English, Wlad was finally accepted and even won a scholarship.

After graduation, he became a noted Hollywood film composer. Then he decided to created his own video game, despite not knowing anything about computer programming, graphic design, or animation. Wlad taught himself all the skills he needed to develop his video game, doing all the programming, all the artwork, all the animation, and all the music himself. His video game, DARQ, won numerous awards and became the #42 most shared PC Game in 2019.

Life will never be fun all the time. Sometimes you may need to do something that you may not want to do in order to get what you do want. As long as you can keep moving closer to your goal, you can tolerate practically anything.

Having passion is the first step. Trusting yourself is the second step. The third step is knowing that whatever you do by following your passion is a success in itself.

Far too many people believe that success must be measured, often by dollar amounts or by popularity. Yet life isn't about winning or losing. It's also not about defining success as a grand slam like creating the next Google or Facebook, or becoming a top

A-list actor or musician. Sometimes success can be as simple as just enjoying your life every moment, every day.

When you avoid defining success as either a massive win or complete failure, you can realize there are many levels of success. Just finding your passion is a major success. Trusting yourself to pursue your passion is another major success, whether you can spend a little or a lot of time doing it. Now any amount of monetary success you achieve pursuing your passion is a bonus.

You may make nothing following your passion or you may become the next multi-millionaire, but it doesn't matter as long as you're engaged in an activity you love and you get to spend as much of your time possible doing it.

That's the true measure of success.

Mark Twain said, "Find a job you enjoy doing, and you will never have to work a day in your life."

Imagine spending every day doing exactly what you love. Now imagine spending every day doing something you don't like, that doesn't inspire you, and that just feels meaningless and pointless.

Which life would you rather live?

Your dreams are within your reach, but only if you're willing to find your passion, trust yourself, and blaze your own trail through life, measuring success as the amount of time you can spend doing what you love and being with the people you love.

Takeaways: If you own too many possessions, your possessions soon start owning you. Possessions alone will always be far less valuable than positive relationships with the people you love. True success is living your life the way you want, mistakes and all.

THE PRINCIPLED PHYSICIST

By Gerald Fisher

Walter Meyerhof was one of my closest associates in nuclear physics and one of the first people I ever worked with. Although I don't think he was well known in the department, I found him to be a man with high principles and a great deal of integrity.

For example, he believed his kids should go to public school, not private school. He did not believe in living on campus, so he lived off campus. He sent his kids to the neighborhood school where he was living. He just had these rules that he lived by. Be reliable and always tell the truth.

I can't say I duplicated his traits, but knowing he was around, interacting with him, and seeing his behavior made me a better person. It made a lot of people better and they probably didn't even know it.

He wasn't perfect. He had his own way of doing things. When we were doing the first nuclear experiment I had ever done, Walter said to me, "I'm going to dinner," and he never came back.

The next morning, after I had worked through the night, I tested everything but the data didn't look right. When Walter came in, I asked him, "You left me alone here all night. Was there an emergency?"

He said, "No emergency. I just thought that it was good for you."

"Good for me? I didn't know what I was doing."

"That's the way you learn," he said.

"I could have hurt someone. I could have radiated people."

He just shrugged and said, "You looked like you knew what you were doing so I trusted you."

A couple of days later around 9:30 a.m., he said, "I have an appointment at 10 o'clock. I'll be right back." And he took off. Ten after 10, he came back. I said, "That was a short appointment. Must have been a short meeting."

He said, "The fellow never showed up."

We continued working. Five minutes later, this undergraduate came into the laboratory and meekly asked, "Is one of you Professor Meyerhof? I had a 10 o'clock appointment with you."

Walter said, "But you didn't show up."

The student said, "I had trouble getting here."

Walter said, "A 10 o'clock appointment means 10 o'clock." The look on his face meant there was no room for debate, so this poor student turned around and meekly walked out of the room.

After he had left, I said to Walter, "He's probably a freshmen. It's the first week of classes. He didn't know exactly where he was going and probably got lost. Plus, he was only 15 minutes late."

Walter said, "If he knew he was uncertain, if he knew the place was going to be a bit mysterious and unknown that he might lose his way, he should have started a half an hour early."

(continued)

(*continued*)

Then I said something stupid. "That's awfully German of you."

First of all, it's a stupid thing to say. Second, to say that to a professor in the department when you're just beginning your career as a second year student is even dumber. Yet Walter wasn't offended. "It has nothing to do with being German. It has to do with being on time."

That's the type of person he was. He taught me lessons without ever needing to lecture me. Another time we were both heading up to the lounge area to get a cup of coffee. He put a quarter into the machine but the machine didn't take his quarter and dropped it in the return slot. He tried it three more times but never got it to work. I put my quarter in and the coffee machine worked perfectly.

I said there must be something wrong with your quarter. When I looked at it, I saw his mistake. "You were putting a Susan B. Anthony dollar coin into the machine," I said.

Walter looked at the coin. "This is a dollar? It's virtually identical to the quarter. You have to stare intently to tell the difference." Then he said, "It must have been designed by a committee," and left it at that.

Another time, Walter and I were walking down the street. Being a first-year graduate student at 20 years old, I was in a shirt, shorts, sandals, completely unshaven with hair all over the place. I looked over at a side street where there was a fire station and I saw the firefighters playing volleyball. Of course I had to say something, and I said, "Is this where our tax money is going?"

One of the firefighters looked at me and replied, "*You* pay taxes?"

Of course, Walter had a good laugh at my expense.

The best experience I had involving Walter was at my thesis defense. Professor Meyerhof was on my committee, along with four other professors as well as 50–60 people in the room to show support. At one point, I showed a drawing that measured a fluctuation that went up and down like a wave.

I pointed to each fluctuation and noted that I had measured them three times. I mentioned that these had to be individual states in the system that I was measuring.

Professor Meyerhof said, "Do you really think those are individual states?"

Stupidly, I said, "Well to the trained eye."

For a graduate student to say that to a professor in the department, especially to someone as well known as Walter Meyerhof was simply disrespectful and stupid.

Walter didn't take it that way. He just said, "Or to the *untrained* eye."

I learned a lot from Walter Meyerhof more than just physics. I learned about how to behave and deal with the ups and downs of life. I'm certain my life improved noticeably from knowing Professor Walter Meyerhof, and I think everyone else in the group benefited in a similar way from his stern but caring personality.

CHAPTER 7

Overcoming Failure

If you've ever eaten at a KFC (Kentucky Fried Chicken), you've probably seen the smiling face of their founder, Colonel Sanders. Despite starting and running one of the earliest successful restaurant franchises in America, Colonel Sanders was a failure for most of his life. He once ran a ferry that was put out of business when a nearby bridge was built nearby.

Then Colonel Sanders ran a gas station in Corbin, Kentucky, that barely turned a profit. To help pay the bills, Colonel Sanders started cooking and selling fried chicken meals, which provided him with his first taste of success that lasted nearly a decade. Eventually, he dumped the gas station and focused solely on running his restaurant.

Unfortunately, a major interstate highway was built that bypassed his restaurant by several miles. That meant all the road traffic he relied on to bring customers to his restaurant would switch to the interstate highway and never see his restaurant at all. After traffic to his restaurant dwindled, Colonel Sanders had to sell his restaurant at a loss.

With no money other than his meager savings and a $105 monthly Social Security check, Colonel Sanders had every reason to doubt himself. His whole life had been one failure after another, and now as a retired man, his prospects for finding a new job was close to nothing. The only true asset he owned was his chicken recipe that people loved, so Colonel Sanders started driving across the country, looking for restaurants that might be interested in using his chicken recipe in return for paying him 5 cents for every chicken dinner sold.

Colonel Sanders had every reason to give up, but he didn't. The reason Colonel Sanders succeeded had nothing to do with luck, intelligence, his background, or his education, all of which were actually working against him. Colonel Sanders succeeded only because he knew how to handle and overcome failure.

What stops so many people from pursuing their dreams isn't other people or outside circumstances. Instead, what stops most people from succeeding is themselves.

You can ignore what other people say. You can avoid or deal with unpleasant situations. What you can't ignore or avoid is your own negativity.

Like Dr. Jekyll and Mr. Hyde, you are a split personality. On one side, you yearn for a better life. On the other side, you also cling to safety and security. That's like trying to swim without letting go of the side of the pool or trying to go skydiving without leaving the airplane.

While the dreamer side of you can always imagine a brighter future, the security-minded side of you always looks for ways to keep you safe. There's nothing wrong with safety except when safety keeps you from trying anything new and different at all.

THE OBSTACLE OF HABITS

If you want to change your life, you must do something different from what you're doing today. Your past actions created the life you have today so if you continue doing what you're doing, you'll just get more of what you already have.

However, if you want something different, you'll have to change, and that means developing new habits. Habits are simply repetitive behavior that you often do without thinking. At one time, a habit likely did something useful for you, which is why you created that habit initially and continue following it.

Habits are neither good nor bad. What matters is whether a habit gives you the results you want. In many cases, if you want something different, you'll have to either develop a new habit and/or get rid of an existing habit. Because habits define who we are, breaking habits or creating new habits can feel like you must literally change into a different person, and that can be much harder than you might think.

One reason why so many people struggle with addiction of any kind (drugs, alcohol, sex, gambling, etc.) is because their addiction has become a habit. Eventually, if you cling to a habit long enough, that habits defines your identity. Even though people may not like or want the results of their addiction and habits, they cannot change because that means literally having to abandon their image of themselves.

Addictions represent the extreme of habits, but all habits define who you are. Habits, no matter how destructive, are familiar and thus comfortable. No matter how much an alcoholic might want to break their drinking habit, until they are serious about putting that addiction in the rearview mirror, they'll always feel comfortable inside a bar surrounded by other people who enjoy drinking. Breaking a habit means changing who you are, what you do, where you go, and even how you think. It's not easy, but it is possible.

All of us have habits. The key is to identify those habits that help you and change or drop those habits that do not help you or that actively work against you.

The first step to creating a new habit or breaking an existing habit is to focus on the change that you want. As long as you keep that ultimate goal in mind, you can constantly remind yourself why you want to change. If you can't see a reason to change, you probably won't change. When you constantly remind yourself of your reason to change, then you'll greatly increase the chance that you will change.

This can be particularly powerful if you link your new habit or the breaking of an old habit to someone you deeply care about. It's easy to get discouraged when you feel like changing your habits only affects you. It's much easier to overcome discouragement when you feel like your loved ones depend on you to change your life for the better.

Alcoholics Anonymous was formed by people with little formal training. They simply discovered a key rule for changing someone's habit. In most cases, people follow a habit based on a trigger, and their habit gives them a reward based on that trigger.

For example, a trigger for an alcoholic might be feeling stress or anxiety at work, or having a fight with their spouse. The reward is to forget their problems by getting drunk. All habits start by triggers where a particular habit is a consistent way a person deals with that trigger to get a reward.

Because that reward feels good, it soon becomes the default behavior for responding to similar triggers. Over time, that habit becomes ingrained, almost like a reflex.

What Alcoholics Anonymous discovered is that you can never eliminate the triggers in a person's life, but you can change the reward they seek to deal with that trigger. Instead of finding solace in alcohol as a reward, Alcoholics Anonymous teaches people to change that reward by going to an AA meeting or talking with a designated partner. By consistently and deliberately choosing a different reward over time, people in Alcoholics Anonymous can change their own destructive habits.

Alcoholics Anonymous also discovered a second powerful motivator by enlisting the help of a friend or partner to keep you accountable. By letting someone else know what habit you want to create or break, that other person can gently remind you when you've slipped and help you get back on track again.

Even better, partners can let you know that it's okay to slip up when you revert back to your old habit that won't help you in any way. Too many times, people view behavior in stark terms as either 100 percent success or 100 percent failure. The truth is that life, even for the most accomplished and successful people in the world, is nothing more than an ongoing series of both successes and failures.

When you pursue success, expect failure. You can never avoid failure no matter what you do. Knowing this, you can expect and plan for failure. No matter how devastating any failure might feel, you can always try again. Failure can never stop you until you allow it to stop you.

Habits define you so it's crucial that you create habits that help you and break those habits that hold you back. The more good habits you cultivate and the more bad habits you cut out of your life, the easier it will be for your life to head in the direction you want it to go.

Here are the top 10 habits that successful people of all backgrounds tend to embrace:

1. Organization

2. Relaxation

3. Action

4. Personal care

5. Positive attitude

6. Networking

7. Frugality

8. Rising early

9. Sharing

10. Reading

Organization is important because it's hard to pursue any goal if you're disorganized and can't find what you need and don't know where you're supposed to be at any given time. Being organized doesn't mean you need to clean your whole house so it looks like a picture in Architectural Digest. Instead, being organized means you can quickly find what you need when you need it. The less time you waste looking for everything from your keys to your important computer files, the more time you can spend actually working toward your goals.

Relaxation might seem like a curious habit to cultivate, but it's all about reducing stress and anxiety in your life. Life events can sometimes overwhelm even the most organized person. Even the daily stresses of traveling, dealing with unpleasant people, and facing minor emergencies such as unexpected work deadlines can derail your progress toward a goal. That's why you need to develop a habit to help you unwind and relax so you don't let everyday stresses get in the way of your long-term dreams.

Action is the most crucial habit to develop because until you learn how to make that first step toward achieving a goal, all the dreams in the world won't do you any good. Action is about converting ideas into tangible, physical progress. Just remember the story of the Tortoise and the Hare. The hare might be faster, but the tortoise plods one step at a time toward a goal and steady progress will beat erratic action every time.

Personal care is about taking care of yourself in the form of diet, exercise, and hygiene. When caught up in a goal, it's easy to put everything and everyone else ahead of your own basic needs. Don't do it. Feeling groggy from lack of sleep or feeling physically unwell from eating junk food will simply be a self-inflicted obstacle that will hinder your progress toward any goal.

If you wouldn't let someone sabotage your dreams, why would you be willing to sabotage yourself? Develop the habit of caring for yourself every day. After all, you're the one who will ultimately benefit.

A positive attitude is crucial because such a state of mind will help you overcome the inevitable obstacles, roadblocks, and outright failure you're sure to encounter no matter what goal you pursue. On the other hand, a negative attitude will cause you to dismiss everything good in your life and focus all your attention on everything bad, even if it doesn't exist. The next time you go to a restaurant and deal with a waiter or waitress, ask yourself would you rather be with someone with a positive attitude or a negative attitude? A negative attitude turns people off while a positive attitude attracts others to you. The greater the positive attitude, the less imposing any obstacles will seem.

Networking is a habit that involves staying in contact with the people you know and developing relationships with new people all the time. Networking means helping other people achieve their goals because then it's likely they'll want and be able to help you achieve your goals. Remember, few people succeed solely on their own. Most people succeed with the help, guidance, and emotional support of someone else. Developing a healthy network of close friends and allies can make tackling even the most imposing project more approachable.

Frugality is more than just spending your money wisely, but also about spending your time wisely as well. Not everyone begins with the same amount of money each day, but everyone, including A-list movie stars, the highest paid athletes, and the most successful entrepreneurs, all begin each day with the same amount of time. What you do with your time determines how tomorrow will turn out. The more time you can spend working toward your dream, the faster you'll likely achieve that dream. Spend your time wisely and you'll be surprised how much you can accomplish in a short amount of time.

Rising early gives you extra time in the morning. You can spend that time doing important work or trivial work that you can't avoid. What matters is that by waking earlier, you can get more out of each day than someone who wakes up far later. Just remember – it's not how early you wake up each morning that counts, but how much sleep you get and how you spend your time when you are awake. Making a habit of getting up early can give you time to do any necessary tasks so you can spend the rest of your day doing something else.

Sharing is all about keeping people in your life who are closest to you. It does you no good to cloister yourself away like a monk and maniacally pursue a goal at the sacrifice of being around anyone else. It's far more important for you to share your time with others along the path to your goal. By making it a habit of sharing part of yourself with others each day, you'll maintain your most important relationships and make your journey just as rewarding as your ultimate goal.

Reading can be one of the most important habits to cultivate. That's because nobody knows everything so the best way to learn anything new is from another person. Since experts in other fields may not be near you, you can do the next best thing and read books written by others. Each time you read a book, you can learn from that author. At the very least, every book can give you one idea that you didn't have before. That one idea can sometimes be the most important idea in the world. By reading regularly, you can expose yourself to different ideas and learn from others far faster than you could ever learn by trying to do it on your own.

Developing good habits can not only make your life easier as you progress toward your goals, but the more good habits you embrace, the less room you'll have for bad habits to take hold. Instead of spending your time watching TV just to pass the evening away, read a good book. Each positive habit you adopt for your own life can make it easier for you to achieve anything you want.

THE OBSTACLE OF SELF-DOUBT

While bad habits can sabotage your efforts to reach any goal, a far worse obstacle is your own self-doubt. Many people doubt themselves and fear failure so they prefer to avoid taking chances. By doing nothing and playing it safe, these people minimize the chance for failure. Unfortunately, they also minimize (or completely eliminate) their chance for success.

If you fear failure, then doing nothing is the fastest way to guarantee the failure that you fear. If you really want to avoid failure, it's far better to strive for a goal because the process of pursuing it will at least give you a chance to succeed.

Combined with the fear of failure is an accompanying thought in people's mind as they wonder, "Am I good enough?"

The answer is always yes and no.

Yes, you are always good enough to pursue any dream, and no, you may currently lack the necessary experience, skills, and knowledge to achieve your dream. Therefore, don't use self-doubt to stop you but use self-doubt to motivate you to become stronger. The stronger you get, the more likely you'll develop the necessary talent to get what you want.

Just remember that everyone started as a beginner at one time. Every gold medal Olympic athlete started as a rookie in their chosen sport. Every multi-millionaire entrepreneur started with just an idea in their industry. Every musician had to learn to play an instrument and sing at a time when more experienced musicians were already further ahead and gaining recognition.

Everyone suffers from self-doubt – even people who have reached the top of their field and wonder how much longer it can last and worry when it will start fading away. Self-doubt is normal. Just don't let self-doubt stop you.

Lady Gaga may seem to be one of the most successful recording artists in history, but even she regularly suffers from self-doubt and low self-esteem. Lady Gaga admitted that she dressed outrageously partly to draw attention away from her real self, a woman named Stefani Joanne Angelina Germanotta. Despite all her fame, power, and wealth, even Lady Gaga questions her abilities.

Any time you doubt you have the right look, talent, skill, experience, or ability to succeed, the answer is that it never matters where you are right now. What ultimately matters is what you're doing today to help you get to where you want to be tomorrow.

THE OBSTACLE OF PERSISTENCE

Anything worth pursuing will take time. While you can easily achieve trivial goals with few problems, achieving more worthwhile goals can take far longer. The longer it takes, the more tempting it can be to simply give up. Don't.

Remember, the journey is far more important than the end result. If you enjoy the journey, then it doesn't matter where it takes you. However, if you're only looking at the end result, then any amount of time will always seem like too long.

As long as you enjoy what you're doing now, you'll always have the persistence to continue toward your goal in the end. In 1979, Jadev Payang saw thousands of snakes and reptiles dying on a barren sandbar after they had washed up on the banks of the river Brahmaputra. From that moment on, Jadev, who goes by the nickname of Molai, devoted his life to preventing other animals from dying in that same way.

For over 30 years, Molai planted trees and even imported ants to create an ecosystem that could thrive on its own. In 2008, the Indian government named his ecosystem the Molai forest, which is now home to dozens of animals, including tigers, rhinoceros, deer, rabbits, and apes.

Molai created his own forest to save animals, so as long as his efforts were helping one animal, he knew he could keep going. Over time, his efforts simply grew until he achieved a nearly impossible dream of making his own forest. That shows the power of persistence.

Any time you feel like quitting, ask yourself if what you're doing right now is worth doing. If so, then you'll have no trouble persisting. If what you're doing right now doesn't seem worth it, it may be time to reevaluate your dreams to see if you need to change your tactics or simply choose a new goal altogether.

Nature doesn't put obstacles in your way to stop you, but to make sure you want your goal bad enough. The more obstacles you overcome, the closer you're getting to your goal, so treat obstacles as milestones that show how far you've come even if you have no idea how much further you need to go. Every problem forces you to reevaluate what you're doing and why. Don't see problems as something to avoid but as something to help you find your passion and what you really want to do with your life so you can make a difference in the world.

THE OBSTACLE OF "EXPERTS"

When you pursue any goal, you're going to run into people with far more experience and knowledge than you. If any one of these experts tells you that you can't achieve your goal, it's easy to believe them. After all, these people are the experts, right?

Wrong.

Just because someone might be an expert doesn't mean they can't be completely wrong. In fact, you'll find that experts can be wrong as often as they can be right. Just ask the film school at the University of Southern California that turned Steven Spielberg down multiple times. Or ask Hewlett-Packard why they turned down Steve Wozniak's early computer design five times. This same design would go on to form the basis for the wildly popular Apple II computer.

Ask 12 different publishers why they rejected J.K. Rowling's first book, featuring a character named Harry Potter, which would go on to spawn a billion-dollar industry incorporating books, film, merchandise, and theme parks.

Why did Walt Disney reject Charles Schultz's cartoons as too simplistic, yet his "Peanuts" cartoon would go on to earn billions of dollars for decades from TV, movie, and merchandising rights? These people were experts – how could they get it so wrong?

While an undergraduate student at Yale, Fred Smith came up with the idea for an air transport system that could delivery packages overnight. Although his economics professor wasn't impressed about his idea, Smith went on to implement this idea that formed the basis for Federal Express.

At age 15, Jack Andraka thought he could create a diagnostic test for pancreatic cancer that would be better than the tests that had been developed by scientists, research labs, and pharmaceutical companies. He wrote a proposal about his diagnostic test, and sent it to 199 research labs. All 199 research labs rejected his idea.

Finally when Jack contacted the 200th research lab at Johns Hopkins University, he found acceptance for his proposal. As it turns out, Jack Andraka's pancreatic cancer test was 100 times better and 26,000 times less expensive than the tests the medical field had been using to that point.

How did a 15-year-old come up with a better and less expensive pancreatic cancer test than hundreds of trained and experienced medical professionals with billions of dollars of funding, years of experience, and access to the latest medical research? We might never know, but we do know that without Jack's dogged persistence, his idea might never have come to fruition and saved countless lives as a result.

The bottom line is that when confronted by less than enthusiastic support or outright hostility from experts in any field, don't let them stop you. Experts can and have been wrong on numerous occasions so there's a good chance they might be wrong about you as well.

Any time an expert tries to shoot down your idea and discourage you that it's impossible, they may be right or they may be completely wrong. Experts are knowledgeable about what already exists. They're often absolutely ignorant about what does not yet exist. Since their expertise derives from knowing what already exists, they cannot be experts on every possible new idea.

So don't let experts discourage you. You may actually know something that they don't. The University of Southern California has one of the most prestigious film schools in the world, yet how many of their graduates have ever achieved even a fraction of the success of Steven Spielberg, who the school rejected?

THE PURPOSE OF FAILURE

In school we're taught to avoid failure with tests that focus on how many questions we got right and how many we got wrong. Yet school can skewer your view of life because tests focus on giving you one chance to get things right. If you fail, your score becomes like a scarlet letter categorizing you at a certain level.

Fortunately, real life doesn't just give you one chance to succeed but a nearly infinite number of chances to succeed. Failure is nothing more than feedback. The more failure you experience, the more you can learn what does and doesn't work.

However, the more you see failure as something to fear or avoid, the fewer chances you'll likely take in the future. Avoiding failure ultimately means avoiding success as well.

Best of all, life gives you time to learn from your mistakes. There's nothing wrong with making mistakes. Nobody can possibly know everything, so any time you try something different, you can't help but make mistakes. The only way you can fail with mistakes is to avoid making them at all, which is impossible.

You will make mistakes. Yet no matter how many mistakes you may make, nothing can ever stop you without your permission.

Life always gives you one more chance. The only question is whether you'll take it.

Actor George Clooney has had a successful career, starring in movies such as *Ocean's Eleven* along with appearing in the hit television series *ER*. Despite all his success, he credits his biggest failure with motivating him to become a better actor.

Back in 1997, George Clooney landed the starring role as Batman in the movie *Batman & Robin*. That movie also featured Chris O'Donnell, Uma Thurman, Alicia Silverstone, and Arnold Schwarzenegger, in what many in Hollywood predicted would become one of the biggest blockbusters of the year.

Instead, the movie bombed and killed the entire Batman franchise for almost an entire decade. That's when George Clooney realized he had just taken the role of Batman for the money, but that movie's massive failure forced him to evaluate his principles.

Did he just want to make money, or did he want to make good movies? His career survived the failure of *Batman & Robin*, and Clooney credits his role in the movie with forcing him to become a better actor.

No longer would he take roles just for the money but because they were part of a good script that told a compelling and important story in the first place.

What type of actor would Clooney had become if he hadn't experienced the worldwide failure of *Batman & Robin*? We'll never know, but we do know that he emerged from his failure to become a better actor, and that might never have happened if he hadn't experienced failure on a massive level.

Most people fear failure because they're afraid if they fail once, it will stop them in their tracks and mark them as a loser forever. First of all, most failures are nothing more than temporary setbacks. Second, nobody wants to be a failure, but the only way you can truly fail is by not learning from your mistakes. Once you make a mistake, no matter how bad it may feel at the time, you can learn what *not* to do. As Thomas Edison said while trying to invent the light bulb, "I have not failed. I've just found 10,000 ways that won't work."

If you want, replace the word *failure* with *feedback*. You need feedback all the time to get better. If you play a sport or practice a craft, you can always get feedback from a more experienced coach or teacher who can help you improve.

Think of a child learning to walk for the first time. The goal is to walk without falling down. The starting point is crawling without knowing how to walk. In between, that child must keep trying to stand up and inevitably falls back down again. The only way to learn how to walk is to fall down.

Nobody ever gets it right the first time.

Everybody makes mistakes. How you react to those mistakes determines whether you'll eventually succeed. If you let mistakes paralyze your progress, you'll never reach your goal. If you let mistakes teach you what not to do, you'll always get one step closer to your goal.

The way to deal with mistakes is to keep your eye on the goal. As long as the goal is something you truly want, and the activity to achieve that goal is something you truly enjoy, you'll have the motivation needed to keep going no matter what.

If you only want the goal but don't enjoy the activity needed to reach that goal, it will be too easy to get discouraged the first time you run into a major roadblock. However, if you enjoy the activity needed to reach a goal, then no amount of obstacles can keep you from continuing that activity no matter how many mistakes or setbacks you face.

The key to defeating failure is passion. Remember, you can only create happiness through action, so as long as you're having fun doing something you enjoy, failure is nothing more than another way to explore how to enjoy your activity even more.

If you don't enjoy the activity needed to reach a goal, then failure can let you know that you might want to find some other activity that you're truly passionate about instead. There's no shame in trying different activities and pursuing different goals to see what you like. You may find you like something as a hobby but not as a career, or you may find what you thought you might like isn't what you really want at all.

In some cases, you may find you're passionate about one topic but equally passionate about something else entirely. People often change careers at least once during their lifetime. That means they switch from one industry to a completely different industry, not just change jobs within the same industry.

Ray Muzyka originally trained and worked as a doctor for two years. Then with two other doctors, Ray founded a video game company called BioWare. After five years of running Bio-Ware as its CEO (while still practicing medicine part-time),

Ray guided the company to launching several successful video games until they caught the attention of Electronic Arts, which acquired BioWare.

Ray Muzyka likely enjoyed medicine, but he also enjoyed programming and graphic arts, so he turned his passion in that field into starting his own video game company. Success in any field is less about the status of reaching a goal and more about the activity of pursuing a goal. If you're like Muzyka, you might enjoy pursuing two completely different fields at the same time.

Ultimately, the only way you can fail is to give up and not try at all. So the best way to avoid failure is to never stop pursuing your dreams, whatever they may be. As long as you continue chasing your dreams, you'll always be a success.

Failure never feels good, but don't let it stop you. Think about the world of dating. No matter who you are, you will get rejected by someone else. Yet few people become monks or nuns the first time they face rejection. Instead, they keep trying until they find that one special person who will make you forget all your failures because you'll be so enamored of your success.

Rapper, entrepreneur, and philanthropist Percy "Master P" Miller said (https://finance.yahoo.com/news/percy-master-p-miller-failure-is-not-the-end-175243885.html), "I think people have to realize failure is not the end, and you can learn from failure. [Success] doesn't happen overnight. Consistency is the key to success."

So forget about all the *nos* you're going to hear throughout your life. All you need is just one *yes*, and that can make all the difference in the world. Once you reach your dream, you won't ever remember all those nos you received anyway.

Takeaways: Habits can help or hurt you. By developing good habits, you can increase your chances of success. No matter what goal you pursue, the path of success is defined by the stepping stones of failure. Failure is nothing more than feedback to help you get better.

THE PHYSICIST WHO HELPED STEVE JOBS

By Gerald Fisher

The one faculty member in all the years that I wished I could have known better was Mel Schwartz. Mel was a gifted scientist, actually a certifiable genius who not only won the Nobel Prize but did so by doing a particularly beautiful and important experiment. He investigated two elementary particles that were thought to be identical and showed that they were distinctly different entities.

He was a direct, straight shooter who displayed this in many ways but especially in one case where he wrote the second best letter of recommendation that I know of. The first best, the best of the best letter that I ever saw, was written for the famous Nicola Tesla, who later on became so famous that Elon Musk decided to name his car company after him. Tesla was a Serb, and his Serbian professor had worked in the United States with Thomas Edison. He wrote to Edison on behalf of Tesla:

Dear Mr. Edison: "I have known two geniuses in my life. One is you, and the other is the young man who stands before you."

You will have to admit that's a pretty good letter of reference. For my money, it is the best that I know of. Short succinct and right to the point!

Mel wrote his letter of recommendation for one of his post docs who was applying for faculty positions. Mel's letter was even more succinct than that of Tesla's Serbian professor. He wrote, "Take him," and signed his name. Interestingly, and perhaps not all that surprisingly, everyone receiving the letter did just that. They each made an offer of a faculty appointment to the applicant.

Some years later, I was working with Mel and Mel was teaching when a young fellow named Stevie approached him to ask if he could sit in on his electricity and magnetism class. Of course, the university really discourages people from sitting in for free alongside others that are paying up to $20,000 in tuition.

But Mel was a physicist and said that was fine with him. So we got to know Stevie a little bit because when he'd come around looking for Mel, Mel often wasn't there. So on those occasions, Stevie would share his questions with us. They were pretty much always about silicon, and to be honest about it, we generally had to look up the answers and postpone the discussion to the next time, so we were always one week in arrears.

Stevie, who later became known by his full name Steve Jobs, completed the class. In gratitude to Mel sometime later sometime later, Stevie Jobs offered Mel $5,000 in cash or $5,000 in Apple founders stock.

Mel Schwartz was definitely a gifted scientist and did a beautiful experiment to win a much-deserved Nobel Prize. Yet in this situation, he told Steve Jobs that he would take the cash, saying he didn't see any use whatsoever for a personal computer. He thought the concept was silly. On top of that, he thought the name they had picked out for their corporation, Apple Computer Company, was idiotic.

I don't know what $5,000 in Apple founder stock would be worth today, 45 years later. Maybe $5B or $15B?

I don't know much about Mel's relationships and whether he inspired his students and colleagues because of his generosity and kindness. But I do know that the gift that he had for science and his integrity and honesty and straightforwardness really gave all of us a lift.

CHAPTER 8

Choosing Your Role Models

There's an old saying, "Tell me who your friends are and I will tell you who you are." That's because we tend to be like the people we spend the most time with at work, at home, and during our leisure hours. Another way of saying this is, "Birds of a feather, flock together."

The people we hang around with can greatly influence who we are, but a far more important measurement is who our role models might be. Role models are typically someone you admire or aspire to emulate. That's why so many people admire and respect movie stars, athletes, business leaders, and celebrities of all kinds. Not only do people admire their favorite role models, but they also want to become like them as well.

That's why you must choose your role models carefully.

I sold my company, Bharosa, to Oracle in 2007. Although I respect Larry Ellison, the CEO of Oracle, as a businessman, he is not my role model.

Larry Ellison has been married and divorced four times. While his romantic relationships are none of my business, his lifestyle is not one I aspire to. I neither need nor want his massive fortune or the power he wields as one of the richest man in the world if it means I would have to take time away watching my daughter grow up or miss having dinner with my family every night. There's no amount of money and power that can tear me away from spending more time with my family.

I have enough money that I can spend my time sharing my life with my wife and daughter without any sacrifices whatsoever. To me, that's worth far more than adding more zeroes at the end of my bank account or spending so much time running a business that I never get to enjoy a simple moment like riding a bike with my daughter to take her to school or waking up every morning to eat breakfast with my wife.

Role models can show you what's possible because they've already achieved what you want. Living role models can give you advice personally if you ever meet them, or indirectly through their words and actions. Role models who have passed away can still inspire you through their life stories, their thoughts captured in books, or their stories on what they had done when they were alive.

Role models can show you that if one person can achieve a dream similar to your own, then it's possible for you to achieve that same dream, or even greater, in your own lifetime. For that reason alone, role models can be invaluable because they show what's possible if you only follow in their footsteps.

However, just as role models can show you what you can do too, be cautious in who you admire and who you choose to emulate.

Just because someone achieves great success financially, artistically, or athletically doesn't mean that they may be the type of person you want to become. You may want to achieve the same level of success, but you may not want to achieve that success the same way your role model did it.

Far too many role models in society have money, fame, and power to go along with their carefully crafted public image, but if you peek underneath, you may be shocked at what you might find.

TYPES OF ROLE MODELS

Everyone grows up with role models. As children, we emulate the people around us when we're learning to walk, talk, and behave. When we're young, we spend the most time emulating the people caring for us because that's all we can see and know about the world.

The earliest role models everybody follows are those closest to you such as your mother, father, brother, sister, cousin, uncle, aunt, neighbor, or friend. When you personally know a certain person you admire, you can get first-hand experience studying what they do and how they react in all kinds of situations. Such intimate knowledge is impossible to do with high-profile celebrity role models who you may only know through TV, movies, websites, or concerts.

The second type of role models are those you see from your environment. They may be teachers, coaches, local business people, or local celebrities such as radio or television personalities. These type of role models can offer a different perspective on life than your immediate family role models so that you might see traits and behavior that's totally different from your normal world.

The third type of role models are the international ones known all over the country or even the world such as movie stars, musicians, authors, or entrepreneurs. You may never meet, let alone see, any of these role models except through videos, movies, magazines, or social networks. Yet some of these role models can be more influential and seem more accessible than your own parents or siblings.

Most likely, you'll have all types of role models throughout your life. As you grow and change, you'll likely switch and follow different role models as well. Younger people will likely find someone like Rihanna or Justin Bieber an appealing role model, while older people might choose someone like Abraham Lincoln or Oprah as their role model. Such notable role models offer the greatest success that can aspire you to strive for your own equally ambitious goals.

Everyone has role models who can show you how to talk, dress, think, speak, and behave. By following your role models, you can change and shape your own life to be more like the people you admire.

Just be careful.

One problem with role models is that you may not be able to judge their behavior and actions correctly. For example, it's easy for a child to admire their mother or father and want to grow up to be like them. Unfortunately, some children grow up with less than admirable parents. As a result, it's far too easy for those children to admire their parents and not realize that their parents aren't decent role models after all.

If you just look at the people around you or the people most popular in the news and gossip magazines, it's easy to choose people you know (or think you know in the case of celebrities) as your role models. But that kind of thinking is like standing in front of a dumpster in an alley and trying to decide which chunk of rotting food you want to eat. In that case, all choices may be bad and you risk simply choosing the least awful item. Similarly, if you limit your role model choices only to people you know, you risk choosing the least awful role model that you know about.

A far better solution isn't to look at the people around you and choose the best role model you can find because that forces you to choose from a limited number of options. Instead, a far better solution is to identify the behavior, traits, and admirable qualities you want to develop in yourself. Then find the people who embody those qualities.

Start by deciding what you want. That involves defining your goals and your passion, because without a goal and without knowing what you're passionate about, it's far too easy to get distracted into chasing after money, fame, or power. When you chase after external symbols of success, you'll never find what you're looking for any more than chasing after pictures of food will ever satisfy your hunger.

Once you know what you want, you must look inward to identify what qualities you're lacking. No matter how talented, skilled, educated, or trained you may be, you can always do better. In many cases, you need to identify those personal qualities you either lack or need to improve. That means being open and honest about your limitations and knowing that you must overcome them if you hope to succeed.

After you identify your weaknesses, look for people who have strengths in those areas. Then you can use them as role models to determine how they developed that strength.

For example, many aspiring basketball players dream of reaching the professional leagues. Yet no matter how good you may be at playing basketball, there will always be some aspect of your skills that could use improvement. While coaches can help, role models can inspire.

During the 1980s, a Boston Celtics player named Larry Bird became a superstar. While others may have had more natural talent, Bird simply outworked and outpracticed everybody. He would spend hours practicing basic skills by dribbling a basketball up and down the steps in the stands or practicing shots from all points on the court. Bird may not have been the most naturally gifted player, but he was one of the most determined players, and his persistence and dedication to improving himself made him the superstar he became.

So if you wanted to get better at basketball, you could use Larry Bird as your role model. Spend hours taking shots from all points on the court. Spend hours dribbling a basketball up and down the stairs. By finding the best person who embodies the qualities you want and choosing that person as your role model, you can not only get the best possible role model, but you can avoid choosing mediocre role models by mistake.

You must choose the best role model possible by first identifying the skill or behavior you need for yourself, and then finding someone who can teach you how to develop that skill or behavior. You may never need to emulate any other behavior from your chosen role model, but studying just a single habit from your role model will be more than enough.

APPEARANCES VS. BEHAVIOR

Since role models can help you define who you are and what you want to do, take care to choose only positive role models to emulate. Far too many people slavishly follow influencers like Huda Kattan, Zack King, Joanna Gaines, or Gigi Hadid because they're attracted to their glamorous lifestyle, money, and fame. However, it's far too easy to focus on outer appearances and ignore their far more important behavior issues. You might want to look like your role models, but they don't all have behaviors that are worth emulating.

There's a huge difference between appearances and behavior. Appearances are nothing more than possessions that anyone can get whether it's buying a brand name dress or getting plastic surgery to look more like the role models you admire. For the right price, anyone can mimic the appearances of their favorite role models.

What's more crucial is identifying your role model's behavior. Years ago, it was easy to idolize a rock star or actor and know nothing about their personal life and whether they were charitable or narcissistic. Now, though, when the internet never forgets, influencers are sometimes exposed as having made unwise or unkind choices. Do you want to emulate their behavior? How does their example help you become a better person, reach your goals, or align with your principles?

If you can't answer that question, you might be seduced by a role model's carefully crafted persona and not realize you're actually admiring an illusion. Between Photoshopped doctored images, plastic surgery, and an army of makeup artists who specialize in making celebrities look good in front of the camera at all times, it's easy to mistake appearance for reality.

Even many celebrities do not look exactly like their own pictures on the covers of magazines like *Vogue*. That's because images are shaped for perfection, and no one can look perfect at every moment. So those images and videos you see of your favorite role models are nothing more than a carefully constructed illusion to make you think someone is more beautiful, more handsome, or more perfect than anyone else on the planet.

There's nothing wrong with admiring someone else, but you must remember that admiring phony perfection is no different than admiring the cartoon images of Snow White or Cinderella from the old Disney movies. Cartoon images aren't any more real than the phony images of the latest YouTube star. When you seek to emulate an illusion, you can't help but feel disappointed that your own appearances can never match their illusionary perfection.

That's a recipe for disappointment, depression, and ultimately low self-esteem.

When you compare yourself to a fantasy, there will always be some better looking, richer, and more famous than you. Even in real life, there will always be some better looking, richer, and more famous than you. Any time you compare yourself to others, you can always see how you will come up short.

Rather than admire the results that major celebrity role models present to the public, focus on the actions that made these celebrities such sought-after role models in the first place. When you ignore the outer appearance of glamour and wealth and focus on the behavior and actions that generated that glamour and wealth, now you'll be able to identify steps you can follow to achieve those same type of results.

You don't want to emulate a role model's public image or persona because that's likely not even real. You want to emulate a role model's behavior. Ideally, a role model's behavior will show you how that person achieved success. If a role model's behavior fails to show you how to achieve success in any form, then you're likely following the wrong role model.

Many people look at Walt Disney as a role model. Even though few of us may want to start an animation studio or run a theme park, people admire Walt Disney for his vision and drive. Despite multiple business failures, Walt Disney had a vision to offer family entertainment through cartoons.

Throughout his life, people told Walt Disney no. Even his own brother, Roy Disney, tried to stop Walt from building Disneyland because he feared it would flop and bankrupt the company. Walt Disney isn't a role model just because he was successful but because he held on to his vision and he found a way to achieve that vision and make it into a reality.

Anyone can emulate the courage, determination, and persistence of Walt Disney to achieve any goal. Any time you experience doubt about choices in your life, you can ask yourself, what would your favorite role model do in that same situation?

Would Walt Disney sacrifice his principles to make a quick buck? Or would he hold on to his principles and find a way to achieve his goal despite any lack of financial or emotional support from anyone around him? When you use a role model as a measuring stick to help guide your life, your own journey through life won't feel as lonely or uncertain.

Now consider a different role model who flaunts a luxurious lifestyle on internet videos. If you examine that person's behavior, you might not find any principles at all beyond partying, flaunting wealth, and having a good time. Put that person in a dilemma and ask, "Would that role model sacrifice his or her principles just to make a quick buck?" Whatever answer you come up with will tell you what type of role model that person really is. Once you know what a particular role model might do in questionable circumstances, you can decide if that's the type of person you want to be as well.

THE ROLE MODELS IN BOOKS

There's a saying that if you read just five books on any topic, you'll know more about that topic than the vast majority of people in the world. So don't limit yourself to emulating role models of people you can see. You can often learn the best thoughts and practices of people through books different role models may have written or through books written about them.

Best of all, books can capture the knowledge, experience, and thoughts from people in the past or people you may never get a chance to ever meet in person. Even better, you can constantly review books to refresh your role model's wisdom wherever you go.

Unlike personal role models who may not be readily available, books can provide information, guidance, and advice to help you in all aspects of life from people you may never meet in real life. You can check out books from libraries for free, or purchase books inexpensively online. Even better, many of the best books are now available as digital ebooks, which means you can literally carry thousands of the best ebooks wherever you take your smartphone or tablet.

Remember, books capture a role model's important advice and information, but whether you get guidance from a book or a living person, even the best information in the world will be pointless if you don't apply it to your own life.

The goal of any role model is to change your life somehow and nudge it in the right direction. Initially, such gradual pressure may seem like nothing is happening but just as braces can realign even the crookedest teeth, so can steady and consistent pressure gradually change your life for the better.

You may never be able to spend time with your role models but you can always spend time with a good book. Best of all, books often reference similar books, so you can discover authors and other role models you might never have known about otherwise. Get in the habit of reading to learn how you can move faster, easier, and more efficiently toward whatever goal you set up for yourself. Your library is the best free source that anyone can use. You just have to take that first step and walk through the doors.

POSITIVE AND NEGATIVE ROLE MODELS

There's a story about two twins who grew up with an alcoholic father. When these two twins left home, one of them became an alcoholic. When asked why he became an alcoholic, he replied, "I grew up with an alcoholic. How could I turn out otherwise?"

Yet the second twin was not an alcoholic but a successful and happy businessman. When asked why he did not become an alcoholic like his twin brother or his father, he replied, "I grew up with an alcoholic. Why would I want to turn out like him?"

This story demonstrates two points. First, role models can be either positive or negative. Second, whatever role model you choose, the way you turn out depends entirely on how you think and react.

The first twin saw his father as a positive role model and decided he had no choice but to emulate that lifestyle whether he liked it or not.

The second twin saw his father as a negative role model and decided he could choose not to emulate that lifestyle because it wasn't the way he wanted to live.

So not only can role models be someone you admire and want to emulate, they can also be someone who represents all the negative aspects of life that you want to avoid.

Suppose you want to start your own business. It's easy to look at people like Bill Gates or Elon Musk as a role model for someone you can mimic, and that's fine because both men represent successful entrepreneurs. Now take a moment to find a negative role model who is the type of entrepreneur you don't want to become.

While attending Stanford's School of Engineering, Elizabeth Holmes decided to drop out and use her tuition money to start up a health care technology company called Theranos. Holmes looked up to Steve Jobs as a role model, even going so far as to dress in a black turtleneck sweater like Jobs did. Although she wanted to become the next Steve Jobs in health care technology, she failed to emulate Jobs's ability to create successful products.

Instead, Holmes raised millions of dollars in venture capital while promoting her company's blood-testing technology. Unfortunately, her blood-testing technology did not work, which led her to deceive investors and partners alike.

As a role model, Holmes can show you what *not* to do. Mainly, do not deceive others (be honest). For anyone wishing to become an entrepreneur, Holmes can show you how not to behave.

It's important to have more positive role models than negative ones, but negative role models can serve as a warning for how you do not want to behave. Just remember that what you think about and focus on the most tends to shape who you become as a person. As James Allen said in his book *As a Man Thinketh*:

Mind is the Master power that moulds and makes,

And Man is Mind, and evermore he takes

The tool of Thought, and, shaping what he wills,

Brings forth a thousand joys, a thousand ills: –

He thinks in secret, and it comes to pass:

Environment is but his looking-glass.

In other words, if you focus on positive role models, you'll tend to develop those traits and qualities of your positive role models. However, if you focus on negative role models, you risk developing those traits and qualities of your negative role models. So use negative role models as a warning beacon but keep your thoughts clearly focused on your positive role models. It's far easier to steer in the direction you want to go rather than constantly avoiding all the directions you don't want to go.

ROLE MODELS ARE NOT REAL

One key point about any role model is that they're not real. That's not to say they aren't real people, but that you can never truly know how any of your role models think or feel, even those role models closest to you such as parents, siblings, or relatives.

When choosing a role model, you'll always be seeing just a part of a person. Use that part to help you become a better person, but realize that emulating the behavior of someone might never help you develop the full qualities you may admire in that person.

For example, many people admire Tim Cook, who became Apple's CEO after Steve Jobs passed away. One habit of Tim Cook is to wake up early and start dealing with email messages as early as 4:30 a.m. By 5:00 a.m., Tim Cook is in the gym, and that's how he starts his day.

That habit works for Tim Cook but waking up at that exact time and going to the gym at 5:00 a.m. may not work for you. Tim Cook's habit is to get an early start each day so he can focus the bulk of his day on important tasks while making sure he deals with less important but still necessary tasks (replying to email) and taking care of his own health (going to the gym).

If you're going to use Tim Cook as a role model, focus less on the specifics of his behavior and more on the results. In his case, he wakes up early to make sure he has enough time to take care of his health and his daily work. You may prefer to go to the gym at night or in the afternoon and sleep in until 10:00 a.m. every day. The details of your role model matter far less than emulating the tasks and discipline needed to get the desired results.

It's okay to admire role models but keep in mind that they're just people too, just like you. You don't want to worship role models but simply respect and emulate their best qualities. By adapting different role models' traits into your own life in your own way, you can eventually create the best version of yourself that you can be.

ROLE MODELS ARE NEVER PERFECT

No matter who your role model might be, critics will be able to find flaws in their past and their behavior. Many people look up to Ghandi for his nonviolent protests in freeing India from

British rule, but critics can rightly point to Ghandi's less-than-admirable behavior in mistreating his wife, fighting with his son, and holding racist views against others.

Many entrepreneurs use Steve Jobs as a role model for his role in shaping Apple into a technological giant that builds products to make people's lives easier. Steve Jobs once referred to personal computers as "bicycles for the mind" because he learned that nearly every animal was more efficient at moving than humans. However, when a human pedaled a bicycle, they were more efficient at moving than any animal in the world.

Despite Jobs's vision for technology, he also was known for intimidating employees and treating them harshly. Steve Jobs also denied his own daughter for years and refused to provide financial support for both his daughter and her mother for years, despite being a multi-millionaire.

Since no role models can ever be perfect, don't worry about finding the "perfect" role model because there will never be one. Instead, focus on the admirable qualities you want to emulate and acknowledge their flaws that you do not want to embrace.

Even better, embrace several role models who focus on different aspects of your life. For example, you might admire someone like Colin Kaepernick for risking his NFL career to protest against police brutality and racial inequality. Kaepernick can help strengthen your ideas that principles are worth more than ignoring problems just to make money.

You might also respect Pulitzer Prize–winning novelist and poet Toni Morrison for being the first black woman to receive a Nobel Prize in literature. Morrison can inspire you that just because nobody has yet achieved a certain level of recognition (no black woman won the Nobel Prize in literature before her), any goal is not impossible regardless of any racial barriers you may have to break through.

Role models are people so acknowledge their flaws and limitations. Then focus on their admirable qualities that have led them to achieve a certain level of success. By picking and choosing the best qualities from different role models, you can become the type of person you want to be and pursue the dreams you want to achieve.

Role models may be amazing people, but always remember that you can reach their same level of greatness, too. Role models can show you the way to your dream and one day, you may find yourself becoming a role model to others.

BE A ROLE MODEL FOR YOURSELF

When most people think of role models, they think they need to look outside of themselves for inspiration. However, don't overlook yourself. Not only can you inspire others (and thus feel the satisfaction of guiding others toward their own goals), but you can also find ways to make yourself proud of who you have become.

Remember, use other people as role models to guide you, but never compare yourself to others. Instead, only compare your progress with your past self. Keep a journal and track what ways you're working on to improve yourself and jot down moments when you notice a change.

For example, you might want to become more sympathetic to others and not so self-centered. When you keep this goal in mind, you can jot down those times when you were more selfless toward others. The more times you record yourself behaving in the way you want to become, the more inspirational it can be to see how much you've changed over time.

By becoming your own best role model, you can constantly strive to become the best you can be. Now no matter what happens, you can look back and see how far you've come. Seeing your own progress over time can motivate you to keep going, because you'll clearly see the results in your own life.

So think of what type of person you want to become, and then start behaving the way that your future, ideal self would behave. There's nothing more satisfying than to look in the mirror and truly respect who you see looking back at you despite any flaws and weaknesses. Then you can honestly smile at your own accomplishments with a sense of wonder and delight, that can boost your self-esteem in ways that can never be taken away.

Takeaways: Role models can inspire you to duplicate their success. Just remember that role models are *people*, so you may admire their accomplishments but you may not admire their behavior. Use role models to show you what you can do and what you don't want to do. When you can be your own best role model, you can influence others, too.

THE ENTHUSIASTIC PHYSICIST

By Gerald Fisher

Bill Fairbank was a unique personality who I would comfortably describe as one of the greatest of colleagues. Always there for you, always producing good results. Just a wonderful person to be around who added immeasurably to everyone around him.

Whenever I needed a letter of recommendation, he was always there to volunteer. Normally you would have to ask someone to write a letter of support for you. He was different. He would bump into you and say, "If you need a support letter, don't hesitate to ask. I could write you one that you can take with you now."

That's the kind of person he was. He infused his department and the physics community, maybe even the whole country, maybe even the whole world, with his unbridled enthusiasm. His kindness, generosity, and caring not only didn't hamper his ability to get to the top of low temperature physics but I think significantly enhanced it.

When I became a department head, I was faced with something called the departmental review, which was required every five years and needed two external reviewers to "impartially" review the department and make recommendations.

I was new to the chair position and clearly naive. The review turned out to be pointless; no one read it, and no one acted on it in any way.

I had asked Bill Fairbank to act as one of our external reviewers. What a mistake to waste the time of one of the top low-temperature physicists on a highly inappropriate task. Surprisingly, Bill didn't mind at all. He told me not to worry because he just wanted to help the department in any way that he could.

Some years later, I had the honor to host a conference of quark searchers. Bill, having one of the premier experiments in the search for quarks, accepted my invitation. When I was discussing who I should get as a keynote speaker, Bill said he would be glad to do it.

I said, "You've done so much for me that I can't imagine asking you to do the keynote address."

He said it was not a problem at all. Then he went ahead and delivered the keynote. The conference ran for

(continued)

(*continued*)

four days, and Bill attended every event. He was interested in those talks, but his attendance and dedication to the events certainly helped me and our department.

This was a very special individual whose kindness, gentleness, compassion clearly enhanced his science. I'm not sure when he ever slept. I would come in during an experimental run at around midnight. I preferred the graveyard shift over getting there at 8:00 o'clock in the morning for the morning shift. So I would walk through the door at 11:45 or slightly after 12:00 o'clock and there was Bill's door open and there was Bill.

He would see me and come running down the hall holding some papers in his hand, and he would latch on to me. He always had a research paper with him, and he would spend infinite time telling you that it was the greatest research paper ever written.

He would say, "You have to read this paper. You have to read it right now. It is the greatest thing since Einstein, and it's going to change the whole nature of physics and the whole nature of the world. It's just absolutely transcending, and you just have to read it now."

One time I was on my way to participate in one of the experiments that we were operating. We were doing something tricky and delicate, and I needed the time to concentrate. I truly loved talking to Bill, but this was not a good time. I didn't want to be rude, but I was really pressed for time.

I began to politely inch my way down the stairs toward the laboratory. He followed me, constantly extolling this wonderful paper. I put my books and my papers down on the lab table. I took off my jacket and rolled up my sleeves. It would be quite clear to anyone that this was a work situation that required some concentration and privacy; but not to Bill. He was still there and still talking about his latest game-changing paper.

Once he followed me into the bathroom as he was still extolling me about some wonderful paper. Another time, Bill followed another colleague into the bathroom and into the toilet stall, where he propped himself firmly up against the stall door so that the colleague couldn't close it.

To Bill Fairbank, every research paper that he received or read was the greatest thing ever done. In addition, he made you feel that your work was equally super special.

He was always enthusiastic about everything. That always pumped me up and pumped all of us up in the department. He was a special, caring, nice person because he always thought of others and always wanted to share his enthusiasm with as many people as possible.

Chapter 9

The Importance of Principles

We're all born alone, and ultimately, we will all die alone. Although we may be surrounded by our mother, father, doctors, relatives, and friends through all stages of life, in the end, only we can go through each experience and decide for ourselves how we will react and what we will do next. That means the fate of your life lies solely in your own hands.

That's a huge responsibility, but it's ours whether we like it or not. It's easy to blame others for your problems and take credit for anything good, but that's never the way to success. That path can only lead to delusion, frustration, and anger. A far better solution is to look at reality with wide-open eyes, determine what you like, what you don't like, and then go about fixing the problem.

If your car broke down on the highway, you wouldn't blame the economy, the current politicians, other countries, or people you don't like. Doing so still wouldn't fix your problem of a broken car on the side of the road. Instead, you would focus on getting help to tow your car off the road and into a garage where a mechanic could diagnose the problem and fix it.

That's the way you have to approach your own life, by taking responsibility for making decisions that impact the quality of your life. At any moment, you always have a choice. You can actively work toward achieving positive outcomes, or you can passively wait and hope something good will come to your life.

If you passively wait for others to make your life better for you, you're going to be waiting a long time, and it still may never come to pass.

This is your life. You're the one in charge. The sooner you realize that, the sooner you can start shaping your life the way you want to live. Trust me, the rewards are well worth it.

LEARNING TO TRUST YOURSELF

There's a paradox in life. When we're born, we have to trust others to care for us. Initially, our parents take care of our physical well-being. Later, other people come into our lives to care for us such as teachers, coaches, neighbors, and friends. Throughout our life, we've always been able to rely on others to help us, yet the paradox is that eventually we need to learn to do everything by ourselves.

As a baby, we depend on our parents to feed, clean, and protect us, but that's a task we must learn for ourselves when we grow up. As we get older, we go to school and teachers help us learn reading, writing, math, and history by showing us new information that we might never have seen before. Even then, schools can only teach us so much. Even if you go through several years of additional schooling and get a master's degree and a PhD, there will come a point where you must start exploring, teaching, and learning on your own.

No one is an island; everybody needs to learn from others. However, no matter how much others might teach you, you must choose your own fate in the end.

Aron Rolston loved the outdoors and soon became an accomplished mountaineer. One of his earliest goals was to climb all 59 of Colorado's peaks over 14,000 feet (4,270 m). While Aron initially relied on others to teach him about hiking, rafting, and rock climbing, eventually he became good enough to perform these skills on his own.

Then on April 26, 2003, Aron decided to go hiking alone in a remote area of Utah. Even worse, he didn't tell anybody where he was going, so when he was climbing through a canyon and a boulder crushed his right hand against the canyon wall, he was on his own.

With no way to call for help, Aron had two choices: One, he could wait and hope that someone might stumble on him by chance, despite his remote location in an area where few hikers explored. Two, Aron could rely on himself and find a way to save himself.

After five days with dwindling supplies of food and water, Aron carved his name on the canyon wall and videotaped a goodbye message to his family, since he didn't expect to survive the night. That night, he hallucinated and had a vision of himself playing with a future child while missing part of his right arm. That dream instilled in him the belief that he could survive.

By now, Aron's arm had partially decomposed due to lack of circulation, which allowed him to tear part of it off. Then he broke his own bones and amputated his forearm using a dull pocket knife. Finally, he severed his major arteries and wrapped a tourniquet around the remains of his arm. The entire painful process took over an hour.

Once freed, he still had to rappel down a 65-foot (20 m) sheer wall, then hike out of the canyon all with one hand. Then he had to walk 8 miles to his car. After walking 6 miles, Aron ran into a family who quickly alerted the authorities and gave him food and water. Amazingly, Aron survived the ordeal and wrote a book about his ordeal that was turned into a movie called *127 Hours*, starring James Franco.

Despite losing part of his right arm and spending days of agonizing pain going through a traumatic ordeal, Aron came out of that experience saying, "The tragedy inspired me to test myself. I wanted to reveal to myself who I was: the kind of person who died, or the kind of person who overcame circumstances to help himself and others."

While few of us will ever need to make similar life or death decisions like Aron Rolston did when he cut off his own arm, we must all make crucial decisions on our own one day that will shape our future. Do we get married to a certain person or not? Do we go to college and if so, which college? What type of work will we do? More importantly, what can we do to test ourselves to see what kind of person we will turn out to be?

Just as Aron had to answer the question of whether he would live or die alone in that canyon with his arm pinned beneath a boulder, so does each of us have to face that day of reckoning when we have to choose what kind of life we want for ourselves.

It's easy to drift through life and let others make decisions for us. Yet no matter what choices others might make for us, even with the best intentions, we must deal with the aftermath. Even then, letting others choose the major decisions in your life is in itself a decision. No matter what, you cannot escape the fact that you and you alone are in control of your life whether you consciously choose or let others choose for you.

It's not easy making choices that have life-changing consequences, but here's the secret. The easiest way to make any decisions is to rely on the principles you stand for. Your principles are your bedrock foundation that defines who you are and what type of person you are.

What if you don't know your principles? Then that's the first step you need to take right now.

KNOW YOUR PRINCIPLES

Once you know your direction and goal you wish to achieve, you can reach that goal in any number of ways, but what's most important is how you reach that goal. You could lie, cheat, and steal your way to your goal, and you might actually reach it in a far shorter amount of time than if you might achieve otherwise. Then again, if you lie, cheat, and steal your way to success, you'll likely taint that success by making numerous enemies along the way. So you have to ask yourself if hurting others is worth it if you can reach your goal faster.

How you do anything depends entirely on your principles.

If you have little or no principles, you'll be willing to do anything to get what you want. If you're willing to hurt others for your own personal gain, you have to ask yourself what kind of person you are. Even if you might reach your goal far faster than you might if you had just treated others kindly, will it be worth it? Is your own success worth having if you have to hurt one person? One hundred people? One thousand people? At what point do you draw the line (if ever)?

If you live a life without principles, you'll risk doing anything and everything to anyone. Remember, the key to happiness involves doing what you enjoy doing and spending time to strengthen relationships with those you care about the most.

If you should hurt others to get what you want, you'll be doing neither of the two tasks necessary for happiness. If you aren't pursuing happiness through enjoyment of doing what you love and spending time with those most important to you, then hurting others to achieve a goal won't necessarily make you any happier in the end. In fact, you'll likely be just as unhappy once you reach your goal as you were when you were striving for your goal.

If you can't look in the mirror and admire the person looking back at you, it's time to develop your principles so you can like the person you see in a mirror. When you can't face yourself, that's a sign that you know you've let yourself down so now it's time to identify what you can change to make yourself proud to be you.

Only you know what makes you disappointed in yourself. Identify the root of that disappointment. It might be your dishonesty with others, the way you treat people, or simply your lack of progress toward your goal. Whatever shortcoming you dislike most about yourself, you are the only one who can fix it. That thought alone can give you a tremendous sense of power because whatever you don't like about yourself, you alone can change it, and these three steps can help:

1. Identify what you don't like about yourself.

2. Identify what advantages you get from your current behavior. After all, if it didn't help you in some way, you wouldn't be doing it.

3. Find a way to change your behavior and still get the advantage you want without engaging in your own behavior that you dislike.

That's the dilemma that you face. On one hand, you have obnoxious behavior that you don't like, yet you still do because it helps you in some way. On the other hand, you have to stop this obnoxious behavior and risk not getting the benefits that it brings you, just so you can live with yourself.

At one time, actor Charlie Sheen was one of the highest-paid actors on TV where he made $2 million an episode filming the hit show *Two and a Half Men*. Despite massive fame and wealth, Charlie still wasn't happy. He searched for happiness in drugs and alcohol. He looked for quick relationships with prostitutes. He faced domestic violence charges against his wife. He spent all his time and money partying with people who didn't really care about him. His behavior became so erratic that he eventually got fired from his hit show and gradually lost his fame, money, and friends.

In looking back, Charlie said (https://deadline.com/2021/02/charlie-sheen-looks-back-two-and-a-half-men-winning-comments-10th-anniversary-1234702410/), "All I had to do was take a step back and say, 'OK, let's make a list. Let's list, like, everything that's cool in my life that's going on right now. Let's make a list of what's not cool.' You know what I'm saying? And the cool list was really full. The not cool list was, like, two things that could've been easily dismissed."

That's the tug of war you must face. How do you get rid of behavior that gets you what you want in the short-term but sacrifices your principles and your long-term dreams? That's when you must decide what's more important, getting what you want now or becoming the type of person you respect now and in the future. Surprisingly, it's not an easy choice, but it's one you have to make because if you don't like yourself, it doesn't matter how many benefits you get. At the end of the day, you still won't like yourself, so what choice do you really have except to change your behavior?

DEFINING YOUR PRINCIPLES

Principles are not just your core beliefs, but your boundaries as well. It's impossible to tell someone how they should deal with all types of problems they might face in life, but it is far easier to tell someone principles they can use as a measuring stick when given any type of choice.

For example, religious works, such as the Bible, provide plenty of principles such as "Do unto others as you have them do unto you," "Thou shalt not steal," and "Love your neighbor." Whether you're religious or not, principles from respected sources can help guide all aspects of your life.

You can even look at comic book superheroes to see how they follow principles that define their actions and decisions. Batman never takes a life, even those of his enemies, while Captain

America believes in the American dream of freedom, equality, and justice. You'll never see Batman beat up a helpless child, nor will you catch Captain America taking a bribe. That's because their actions stay true to their principles. The way they respond to challenges while still sticking to their principles makes them admirable role models.

Now look at what happens if you lack principles of any kind. Without guiding principles, you'll risk focusing solely on yourself and your own interests, possibly at the detriment of everyone else around you. Without principles, it's easy to justify lying, cheating, and stealing to reach your goals.

The way to develop principles is to look at what's most important to you in life and what are the best qualities you need to develop in yourself to reach your goals.

First, what's most important to you? Look beyond any superficial possessions or acknowledgement that others can give you and focus on core ideals that you treasure the most like love, friendship, and trust. What are the boundaries you will never cross and why?

For example, when you're in love, what is one action or behavior will you always do? Why? Likewise, what is one action or behavior you will never do when you're in love? Why?

By identifying your deeply seated beliefs and why you hold them, you can define your core principles that define who you are. Make a list of these principles and objectively study them. Are these the type of principles that will help you achieve your passion? If not, why not?

One way to define your principles is to imagine you're surrounded by your role models and your loved ones. Would they approve of your behavior based on your principles? If not, then you have to question your behavior and decide what's more important: not changing and staying the way you are or changing to become a better version of yourself.

The hard question you must face is deciding whether your principles align with your dreams and with the type of person you want to be. If your principles do not help you or others, then you need to question whether you need to change your principles or adopt different ones. Being selfish or intolerant toward others may not cause problems initially, but eventually those type of principles will make it much harder to live a happy and joyful life with others. The saddest person in the world is someone with no one to share their happiness.

To get you started, consider the following principles that can help you, no matter what you may want to do:

- Gratitude – Being grateful for what you have helps you stay humble while also helping you maintain a positive attitude about life.

- Trustworthy – You can only go so far in life without the help of others, so being someone others can trust will go a long way toward working with others.

- Timeliness – Being on time is crucial because that shows you respect other people's time and thus you also respect others as well.

- Forgiveness – Everyone, including you, may make a mistake so it's important to be forgiving toward others when they slip up, too.

- Integrity – Living with integrity means being open and honest so you do the right thing even if no one is watching.

- Responsibility – Be willing to accept responsibility for your actions.

- Patience – Be patient with yourself and with others.

- Faith – When you believe in yourself, nothing can stop you in pursuing any goal you want.

PRACTICE GRATITUDE

Out of all these principles, gratitude might be the most powerful. If you're constantly working for the future, it's too easy to forget about the present. When you forget about the present, you risk ignoring the present riches in front of you right now. When your dream lies in the future, it's easy to feel unhappy because you're focusing on what you don't have. When you reminisce about the past, it's also easy to feel unhappy because you're focusing on what you can never go back to. That's why you need gratitude to bring you back to the present so you can experience the current moment, which is the only place where happiness can ever be found.

You can only be happy in the present because that's the only moment you can experience, and those moments are fleeting so you must enjoy them while you can.

No matter how far or how close you may be toward your dream, be grateful for what you have regardless of how much or how little you might have at the moment. At the simplest level, you have your health. Without your health, nothing else really matters, so be thankful each day for having another day you can enjoy.

Next, be thankful for the most important people around you. Life keeps changing every day, which means the people you love will change so treasure the time you have with them today. Each moment you spend with your loved ones will create a new, happy memory in your life. That's something you can never get back so enjoy it while you can.

Finally, be thankful for what you've already accomplished so far in pursuing your dream. By focusing on where you are right now in pursuing your dream, you can see how far you've already come. Today is another day to move one step closer, so be thankful you have this chance and do what you can to make it happen.

No matter how much or how little you've accomplished, nobody can ever take that away from you. You did it, you took the chance, you put in the time, and you did something that 99 percent of world would never do.

Gratitude helps you enjoy where you are right now. Now no matter what happens, you know you're already a success.

REGULAR PRINCIPLE CHECKUPS

Once you identify and define your core principles, post them near your mirror, computer, or anywhere else you'll see them at least once a day. The idea is to keep reminding yourself of your core principles so often that they become second nature.

Writing down your core principles helps you clarify those ideas in your mind. Reminding yourself of them every day helps solidify those principles in your own life. Yet it's still important to do daily checkups to make sure you're following your principles the way you should.

Just as you can't expect to fill a car with fresh oil and never have to change it again, so you can't expect to write down your principles and never have to worry about them afterwards. Not only must you know your principles, but you must also live them every day.

Whenever you're faced with a decision, remind yourself of your principles and what they tell you to do. Sometimes letting go of your principles might seem like the easiest or safest way out of a dilemma, but stop.

Each time you ignore and fail to follow your principles, those core ideas will get weaker. Ignore your principles long enough and soon they risk becoming nothing more than fancy words on a piece of paper that has nothing to do with the way you conduct your life.

To ensure that your principles remain a crucial part of your life, keep a daily journal and track all the times when you faced a choice. Each time you followed your principles, write it down. Each time you failed to follow your principles, write it down – along with the reason why. By tracking how many times you follow your principles or not, you can identify when you're falling short of your own ideal nature. Now you can start correcting your behavior so you can stick with your principles consistently.

While you may slip up once in a while, you want to reach the point where you stick to your principles no matter what it might cost you. When your principles become part of your identity, then you'll know they'll be there to guide you every step of the way toward your dreams.

ALIGNING YOUR PRINCIPLES WITH YOUR RELATIONSHIPS

It's hard enough to identify and write down your core principles. It's even harder to review those same principles and apply them to your everyday life. Now an even bigger challenge is maintaining your principles with the people closest to you.

That's because the people around you may have different principles than your own. When faced with conflicting principles, you have a choice: You can either give up or change your principles or get the other person to give up or change their principles.

If your principles are important to you, you should never change them for any reason. The only valid reason to change your principles is when you can see beyond a shadow of a doubt that clinging to your principles are hurting you and/or others around you. If that is the case, your principles are at fault so you need to choose better principles.

However, you may find your principles don't align with someone else's principles, which will inevitably cause problems.

This is the time to talk with that person and explain your principles and the conflict they're causing with your relationship. Now it's up to that other person to either change their principles or spend less time in your life altogether.

If your principles are worthy, do not sacrifice them for anyone or any reason. That's when you may need to make a tough decision. Do you continue your relationship with someone who doesn't share your principles or do you change your principles? If your principles are important to you, then they'll likely create conflict between you and another person who doesn't share your principles.

Do you sever your relationship with that person or find a way to maintain it, despite any differences over your principles? That's a choice you have to make, but if your principles are really important to you, then the decision should be clear even though it may not be easy.

If your principles are aligned with your dream and with making you a better person, they are worth far more in the long run than any temporary, short-term gain you may get by ignoring them. Don't do it. The right principles can lift you up. The wrong people can drag you down. Which direction do you want to go?

Don't Sacrifice Your Principles

When you have so many options to choose from, it's easy to weed out the ones that won't seem to work. However, when left with a handful of options that all seem equally valid, how can you choose the right one for you?

That's when you need principles. What do you stand for? What line are you unwilling to cross? What's most important to you? The more clearly defined you know your own principles, the easier it can be to use these principles to filter out the options that you won't even consider even if they appear to help you fulfill your passion much sooner.

Violating your principles is never worth it because when you do that, you betray yourself. If you can't trust yourself, who will? If you can't look at yourself in the mirror with a smile, nobody else will do that either. If you can't sleep at night, why are you choosing options that you know in advance will make you miserable?

Your principles form the bedrock of your self-worth. Once you violate your own principles, you've literally destroyed your life. Don't do it.

If you ever find yourself violating your own principles, stop. Then do whatever it takes to make amends with yourself and everyone who you may have hurt. Your reputation and self-worth is far more important than taking a shortcut to any goal.

You're either following your principles or you're breaking them. There's no in-between, no gray area where you can fool yourself that you're really not violating your principles when you know in your heart that you really are.

Treat your principles as sacred. Given a choice between violating your principles and getting a huge benefit, or not violating your principles and getting a much smaller reward, protect your principles every time. Your principles define who you are. The moment you allow yourself to ignore your own principles, you've literally just given the world permission to ignore your dreams and ultimately yourself as well.

YOU'LL NEVER WALK ALONE

If your principles fail to align with the people around you, you may need to change your life and seek out people who do align with your values. Even if you minimize contact with people who fail to align with your principles, you'll never be alone. That's because you'll soon find others who want to improve their own lives by adopting similar principles as well.

There's a story about crabs in a basket. If you put one crab in a shallow basket, it will use its legs and claws to climb out. However, if you put two or more crabs in a shallow basket, you never have to watch over them.

That's because each time a crab tries to crawl out of the basket, the other crab will drag it back down. No matter how many times a crab tries to climb out, there will always be another crab who will pull it back down again.

That's the same thing that can happen if you surround yourself with negative people. Rather than let yourself get dragged down by others, it's best to separate yourself from negative influences altogether. Then surround yourself with people who share similar principles, so that way you can all uplift each other rather than tear each other down.

No matter what your principles might be, you can always find people who believe in them as much as you do. If you live your principles, you'll quickly find that you'll attract people who share your principles and repel people who don't share your principles. In this way, you'll gradually fill your life with people who can inspire you and spend less time with people who want to discourage you.

No matter where you are on your journey through life, you can always find friends. The key is being willing to minimize or cut old ties that no longer support you and make room for new relationships. It may be lonely at times and frightening, but in the end, you'll never be alone.

MAKING YOUR OWN DECISIONS

Whenever you're faced with a choice, use your principles to guide you into making the right decision. Sometimes this choice will be clear where one choice lets you embrace your principles while another choice would force you to violate your principles. In those cases, your decision should be straightforward.

However, in many cases, you could be forced to choose between two choices that would both allow you to uphold your principles. So which one should you choose?

When making any decision, look for the element of fear in your choices. At the most extreme level, fear can make you stay in a job you don't like because you're too afraid to start your own business for fear you might fail. Any time you're avoiding one choice out of fear and embracing another choice out of security, that's a red warning flag that you could be making the wrong choice.

Fear is a great motivator when your life is in danger. Fear keeps us from running in traffic, playing with dangerous animals, or ingesting toxic chemicals. While fear can keep us physically safe, fear is a terrible motivator for advancing toward your dreams.

Fear holds you back. If you allow fear to control you, you'll only do what you already do and thus never go anywhere or do anything. Fear is the reason why some people stay in a job for 20 years but essentially have one year's of experience repeated 20 times.

When faced with two equally compelling choices that support your principles, look for the choice that seems safest, easiest, and most secure – and then take a serious look at the other choice instead.

I once met a man who graduated from college in 2000 and wanted to go into the New York financial industry. He got two job interviews right away, where the first job interview was with a prestigious financial services company called Cantor Fitzgerald, a well-established firm that had been around since 1945.

Cantor Fitzgerald offered him a generous salary to work in their offices that contained marble floors and expensive oil paintings on the walls. Best of all, the job was not only high-paying, but secure. Not surprisingly, this man was tempted to take this job for instant wealth, status, and security.

However the second job interview took place in a dingy rented building filled with computers propped up on picnic tables scattered around the room. For his interview, this man spent 30 minutes watching people staring at computer screens and saying nothing. This firm was on the cutting edge of the growing day trading industry, but because they were brand new, they could not offer a large salary, they did not have any status in Wall Street, and they offered no security whatsoever.

Comparing a job with an established firm like Cantor Fitzgerald to this fledging day trading firm seemed unfair. The Cantor Fitzgerald job guaranteed so much more, yet this man had doubts. Although the Cantor Fitzgerald offer seemed the fastest and safest route to wealth and status, the day-trading firm offered a chance to enter a new world that could potentially dominate Wall Street.

So despite the lack of any guarantee, security, or even money, this man chose the day-trading job that was located several blocks away from the World Trade Center where Cantor Fitzgerald had their offices on the top floor.

Every day when this man when to work at this day trading firm, he could see the World Trade towers in the distance. That reminded him all that he had given up by not taking the job with Cantor Fitzgerald, yet he was surprisingly happy with his job at the day-trading firm because it seemed far more interesting than the Cantor Fitzgerald job.

Then on September 11, 2001, hijackers flew two airliners into the World Trade Center towers, knocking them down. That's when this man realized if he had pursued the secure, safe, and easy job with Cantor Fitzgerald, he would have been on the top floors of the World Trade towers when they collapsed. By turning away from safety and security, and choosing the day-trading job that offered nothing but excitement and the possibility of a more interesting future, this man literally had made a decision that saved his life.

Now most people will never have to make life or death decisions, but any time you face major life-altering choices, what will you do? Will you play it safe and choose security over challenge? Or will you choose a more interesting option just because it looks like more fun?

Everyone has heard of Amazon but in Asia, there's a similar company called Alibaba, which is worth billions of dollars. When Joseph Tsai met Jack Ma, the founder of Alibaba, Joseph was earning $700,000 a year at a private equity investment firm. Ma offered Joseph Tsai a job working for Alibaba for $600 a year, along with the promise of stock options that would only be worth something if the company succeeded.

Logically, the safest and most secure choice would have been to stay at his $700,000 a year investment job, but Joseph Tsai was intrigued by Jack Ma's enthusiasm and decided to take a chance. Today, Alibaba is a global powerhouse and Tsai is a billionaire.

The moral of the story is simple. When faced with potentially life-altering choices, only you can decide what's best for you. No matter what you choose, be aware of the influence of fear because fear will keep you rooted in safety and security and turn you away from far greater opportunities.

If you truly believe in yourself, you can recover from any failure. In fact, many entrepreneurs have gone bankrupt at least once. However, if you cling to security out of fear, the next time another life-altering opportunities comes your way, you'll be far less inclined to even look at it. Eventually, your life can reach a point where you fail to consider any life-altering choices at all because you're too busy holding on to the illusion of safety and security. At the end of your life, do you want to say that you played it safe or that you lived an exciting life? As Steve Jobs once said, "I don't want to be the richest man in the cemetery." In other words, when given a choice between money and security, or freedom and adventure, which choice do you think will make your life worth living?

Takeaways: No matter what you do, ultimately the responsibility of your choices and your life falls entirely on you. Principles can help define your boundaries so you know what you will and won't do to achieve your goals. Whether you define your own life or let others choose it for you, you're the only one who can reap the rewards and suffer the consequences.

THE MAN WHO SAW THE BOMB DROP ON HIROSHIMA AND NAGASAKI

By Gerald Fisher

In a large group I once volunteered that I thought Luis Alvarez was perhaps the best experimental physicist of the twentieth century. Somebody said, "Well, okay, I won't argue the point, but perhaps it would be better to say the latter half of the twentieth century. I didn't disagree. I mean, Fermi was in the first half of the twentieth century and he did some very fine work and being the best experimental physicist in the second half of the twentieth century isn't bad. Apparently, no one disagreed.

Luis was simply that special. I remember 50 years ago I was interested in the problem of the mass of the neutrino. I was discussing it with Stewart Freedman and he decided, and I concurred that it might be a good idea to have a little seminar series where people could present their ideas and we could discuss them.

(continued)

(*continued*)

The series was scheduled, a large number of colleagues including myself asked for a spot and all of the talks including mine went well. Time was a critical factor, so only a few minutes were allocated for questions after each talk. At the conclusion of the day's festivities, everyone was mulling around extending the discussions that had just formally concluded. I was in a group of about a half dozen when out of the corner of my eye I spotted Professor Felix Bloch headed in my direction. Oh my, oh my, what did I do? What did I say?

He came directly over to me and said, "Jeddy (that's how he pronounced my name), that was a very nice talk, but before going too much further, you really should run it by Luis."

How about that? That was pretty high praise having Professor Bloch tell me to run it by Luis. That was kind of like Toscanini telling Marian Anderson to take care of her voice, saying, "An instrument like yours comes along once every 100 years."

Luis spent his career at Berkeley. He invented the bubble chamber and won the Nobel Prize for that plus some pioneering experiments in elementary particle physics. He also used the attenuation (slowing down) of cosmic rays to "photograph" the inside of the pyramids. He found a number of chambers that had not been discovered, and he was also the person who came up with the idea and proof that a meteor about 10 miles across, struck the Earth, causing a huge cloud of debris to go up and encircle the Earth, causing a nuclear winter that may have caused the extinction of the dinosaurs.

I always used that proof in my classes as an example of what it actually means to prove something. You don't just say it. You provide evidence.

Luis had his own research group at Berkeley that ran the Cyclotron, and then after that the Betatron. His personality infused that group with his prowess and dedication. He was also a damn nice guy, and beyond that, he was a straight shooter.

He held a very strict interpretation of science, requiring if you made a statement, to provide proof. As a result, he had the highest integrity that affected me and hundreds of other people who were training to become physicists.

One time, Luis was scheduled to give a talk, and there were 500 people who intended to squeeze into the lecture hall that could only hold 150 people. The lounge area where we had our refreshments and could get a cup of coffee was so crowded that we couldn't move.

Everyone was excited, and there must have been 50 distinct conversations going on at the same time. At one point, I heard a male graduate student ask in a loud voice that carried over the crowd, "Alvarez? Alvarez? What is he? Is that Hispanic? Latino? Is he from Spain?"

Not one person in the very large crowd knew Luis's background, and interestingly, nobody cared! He was Luis, and who cared if he came from Peru or El Salvador or the moon. I was impressed by that two-minute refrain – nobody cared, and that is precisely the way it should be.

Luis had been in Los Alamos working on the nuclear bomb as part of the Manhattan Project, and it turns out he

(continued)

(continued)

was the only human being to go to both Hiroshima and Nagasaki. He was on the spotter plane following the planes carrying the nuclear weapons. He went to Hiroshima in the plane that followed the *Enola Gay*. Three days later, he was in the plane following the bomber that dropped the bomb on Nagasaki.

When I read this, I almost fell over!

So I went over to Berkeley to see Luis. I asked him, "I read you were the only person to go to Hiroshima and Nagasaki."

He said, "Yes, that's true."

I said, "I've known you all these years and you never mentioned this?"

He said, "I don't want to talk about it."

I said, "You need to talk about it."

He, of course, replied that I should show some respect and mind my own business.

I said, "As you well know, I can't do that, so you have the choice: either give me a few minutes now and get it out of the way or put up with me bugging you every day for the rest of our lives."

Luis showed his characteristically big broad smile and said, "Okay, what do you want to know?"

I said, "You actually saw the goddamn bomb drop out of the plane and fall over Hiroshima?"

"That's right."

"And you saw it go off?"

"Yeah, I saw it go off, and my heart stopped. It was a long trip from the Tinian Island in the Pacific to Tokyo, about six or seven hours. On the way over, it was hectic in the plane. Nobody could sit still. Everybody was jumping up and down. People tried to talk about nothing, but it didn't work. Time did not fly by, and everyone was just nervous.

We had no role in the operation except to observe and take some pictures. But on the way back, everything changed; there was no talking, nobody jumped up and down. Everybody just sat quietly, and no one said a word for the whole flight. It was like a wax museum inside that returning plane.

"It felt to me like the flight was taking two days, with everyone just sitting there in dead silence."

I, and all the people who knew Luis, were elevated by his skill, attitude, and personality. He was a pioneer in kindness, but it was more the example he set for all of us. If you could approach Luis-ness at the 75 percent level, you were doing well and you had a right to be satisfied.

Felix Bloch worked with Luis on a beautiful experiment to discover some properties of the neutron. One day, Bloch said that he didn't enjoy working with Luis. This really surprised me, so I asked him to elaborate.

"Well," he said, "when things were going well and we could work in shifts, I would take the day shift and Luis would take the night shift. I'd come in in the morning to relieve Luis and I'd find he made some changes, all

(continued)

(*continued*)

of which were logical and necessary and beautiful, but he never wrote any of it down in the lab book!"

During my period as department head of the small non-PhD granting department, I thought how nice it would be to have some of these great scientists over to give a talk, meet the department, and meet the students. To my delight and surprise, virtually every Noble laureate that I contacted agreed to come (Luis, of course, was one).

An interesting case came from Maria Goeppert Meyer, who said she would be unable to attend. Her work helped us understand the properties of the nucleus of the atom. Actually, the letter came from her husband, Joseph Meyer, and it read, "Thank you so kindly for the invitation. Unfortunately, Maria will not be able to attend, having passed away in 1972."

I, of course, wrote an immediate letter of apology and embarrassment, to which Joseph responded that I was not to worry. "If Maria were still alive," he wrote, "she would have gotten a good laugh over it."

Luis, of course, agreed to give a talk. In my follow-up letter, I asked if he could come over 15 minutes early to see our quark experiment. Luis agreed, I introduced his talk, and he started by saying, "Your department head (me) demanded that I come over early to see your experiment."

I, of course, demanded no such thing.

Then Luis said, "But I'm glad he did because the department should be especially proud to house such a beautiful and important experiment."

Even in the group of accomplished, considerate, and kind scientists, Luis Alvarez stood out. He was not a member of our department. He was just a visitor and yet his kindness, consideration, and professionalism lifted us up more than I can put into words.

Chapter 10

Dealing with Fear

Many people fear failure, so they avoid taking a chance. By avoiding chances, they also avoid success, which means the fear of failure virtually guarantees that they will fail. Sometimes the biggest failure doesn't appear as a dramatic bankruptcy or mistake in full view of thousands of people. Oftentimes the biggest failure appears disguised as a meek life of anonymity that nobody even knows about.

The fear of failure can paralyze you into inaction, but there's a second fear that's equally destructive and that's the fear of success. Now you might wonder why anyone would fear success, but it makes just as much sense as fearing failure.

When you fear failure, you're afraid of looking foolish and losing what you have. When you fear success, you're still afraid of looking foolish but worried about gaining what you don't have that could change your life in negative ways.

Watch many bands that suddenly hit it big. They rarely stay together for long after that burst of success thrusts them into the ranks of superstardom. Once they achieve the success they always dreamed about, they suddenly feel aimless and directionless. When you've achieved your dream and your life hasn't magically transformed into unending days of bliss and happiness, life suddenly appears empty and meaningless.

The problem doesn't lie in achieving your dreams but in what those dreams meant for you in the first place. In his book *Drive*, Daniel Pink identifies two general types of people and their motivation. He calls Type X people motivated by external rewards such as fame, money, and awards. These type of people pursue dreams for the reward they hope to achieve after they reach their goals.

Unfortunately, once Type X people achieve success and reap the fame, money, and awards they wanted, they quickly find that it's never enough. Their motivation lay in striving for success, not necessarily getting it. No matter how much fame, money, or awards they receive, it will never be enough, locking Type X people in an endless treadmill of dissatisfaction and unhappiness.

On the other hand, Daniel Pink also identifies Type I people who are motivated intrinsically by their activity, whether it's painting, writing, playing music, helping others, or starting a company. Type I people enjoy the journey to success for its own sake regardless of any amount of fame, money, or awards they might receive.

If they do achieve success, it doesn't negatively affect them as much because they still enjoy the activity itself. Since Type I people enjoy the journey, they tend to be happier when they do achieve success, unlike Type X people, who suddenly find success hollow and empty.

So if you fear success, ask yourself how you would feel if you never achieved your dream at all. Would you feel like a failure? If so, then it's likely you're pursuing that goal for the end result instead of for the pleasure the pursuit of that goal gives you. When your only form of happiness comes from external factors such as money or fame, pursuing any goal is no different than chasing an empty illusion.

FEAR OF THE UNKNOWN

Life changes all the time. What often happens is that people used to the old ways avoid embracing the new ways. As a result, they miss out on opportunities that the new way offers because they're too busy clinging to the false security that the old ways provide.

Back in 1875, Aaron Montgomery Ward started a mail-order business selling a wide variety of goods. His catalog of items soon became known as "the Wish Book," offering over 10,000 items that no local store could possibly carry.

Montgomery Wards soon spread across the country as retail stores. Yet just a little over 100 years after its founding, Montgomery Wards failed to take advantage of the internet. While Montgomery Wards originally prospered by selling hard-to-find items by mail, Amazon prospered by selling hard-to-find items over the internet.

Why do companies like Montgomery Wards fail to recognize the future? Most likely, because the future contains the unknown, and it's far safer to keep doing what you're already doing rather than take a chance doing something new. This mentality has doomed every major company from Montgomery Wards, Commodore International, Sears, Polaroid, Kodak, Digital Research, Borders Books, Blackberry, Nokia, Lehman Brothers, and countless more.

It's okay to fear the unknown. It's never okay to avoid the future. As John F. Kennedy once said, "Change is the law of life. And those who look only to the past or present are certain to miss the future."

FEAR OF UNWANTED ATTENTION

The fear of success can also bring you lots of unwanted attention, destroying your sense of privacy. Singer Justin Bieber rocketed to stardom with YouTube videos, but under the constant attention and expectations of the adoring public, Justin began struggling with anxiety and mental health issues. He had legal problems connected to assault and dangerous driving.

Despite all the fame and money celebrities earn, they often miss the simple pleasures of life, such as being able to go anywhere they want without worrying about getting attacked by critics or mobbed by fans.

Success in any form will change your life for both good and bad. If you only focus on the negative aspects of success, you'll rightly fear success and do what you can to avoid it. If you focus on both the positive and negative aspects of success, you'll be able to evaluate whether the benefits of success outweighs the disadvantages.

There's always a price to pay for success. Some people are willing to pay that price while others regret paying that price. The difference depends on how well you handle change and whether you're happy without success. If you are not happy without success, then you likely won't be any happier with success either.

Actress Jennifer Grey had a string of hit movies in *Ferris Bueller's Day Off* and *Dirty Dancing*. Despite this success, she felt self-conscious about the appearance of her nose so she had plastic surgery to correct it.

Unfortunately, changing her nose drastically changed her looks. As Grey put it (https://www.mirror.co.uk/3am/celebrity-news/jennifer-grey-on-patrick-swayze-dirty-1274628), "I went in the operating room a celebrity – and came out anonymous. It was like being in a witness protection program or being invisible."

From that point on, she never achieved the same leading roles and stardom that she had before. She lost her success because of her inability to accept herself. By chasing an image of who she wanted to be through plastic surgery, she lost everything she had worked for and in the end, gained nothing in return.

FEAR OF ALIENATION

When you strive for goals, you immediately set yourself apart from everyone else who is not working toward any long-term goal. That can be lonely and alienate you from your friends, relatives, neighbors, and loved ones.

Unfortunately, when you strive to improve your life and others around you do not share your thoughts, the difference can strain relationships. The hardest solution is to convince everyone around you to improve themselves as well so you can all support and cheer each other on, but that requires everyone to change as well. The easiest solution is to stop striving for a better life yourself and stay exactly the same so you don't threaten anyone around you.

The first choice is ideal but rarely possible, since it involves the cooperation of others while the second choice condemns you to your current life where you never attempt to strive for a better life at all. Here's a third and more appealing option. Find a way to make your success help others.

One reason why people around you may resist seeing you change is that they fear being left behind. To dispel those fears, you need to find a way to keep those people in your life so your success becomes their success as well. When those around you see their lives improving because you're improving, they'll be far more accepting and supportive of your dreams. When people see how change can improve their lives, they'll be more likely to want to help you or even change themselves.

There's the story of a professor who placed a sheet of paper face down on the desks of every student in his classroom. When everyone had a sheet of paper, the professor told the students to turn it over, where they saw a black dot in the middle of a white page. Then the professor asked them to write down what they saw.

After everyone finished this exercise, he read through all the students' essays and found that everyone wrote about the black dot. That's when he told the class that nobody wrote about all the white space around the black dot.

People tend to focus on minor differences without noticing the far greater similarities. When people fear losing you if you change, they're also focusing only on your changes and not on the vast history and background you still share with everyone.

So find a way to stay connected to people and assure them that even though you're changing to reach a goal, you're still mostly the same person you always have been. To many people, change means potential loss so if you can eliminate this fear, you'll go a long way toward maintaining your relationships with the people around you.

If people truly care for one another, they should be willing to work together. Unfortunately, relationships can only work with the cooperation of both parties. If one person refuses to change, that may mean you may need to pursue your own dreams without them. Maybe in the future you can reconnect, but if you let others hold you back, you'll feel nothing but regret and hostility that will never help any relationship.

Ultimately, keep a relationship if it makes you feel good. Otherwise, you may discover that some relationships can and should be cut out of your life if they do nothing but drag you down.

FEAR OF BEING AN IMPOSTER

A common saying in show business is that it takes 10 years to become an overnight success. That's because people often toil in obscurity for years before they suddenly break through and achieve the massive success they've always dreamed about.

However, once people become an overnight success, they often feel like an imposter. After all, they're still the same person they were before they were famous. Now they fear their success won't last, that they don't deserve their success, or that people will see them as unworthy of all the sudden attention.

Those are real fears that have plagued every celebrity. Academy Award winning actor, Tom Hanks, has appeared in multiple blockbuster films and even written the screenplays for several movies. Yet even he said (https://www.business2community .com/strategy/do-you-suffer-from-impostor-syndrome-you-are-not-alone-02324575), "No matter what we've done, there comes a point where you think, 'How did I get here? When are they going to discover that I am, in fact, a fraud and take everything away from me?'"

Noted entertainer Lady Gaga said, "I still sometimes feel like a loser kid in high school and I just have to pick myself up and tell myself that I'm a superstar every morning so that I can get through this day and be for my fans what they need for me to be."

Feeling like a fraud is natural, and something even the most respected celebrities face every day. So if you're feeling like you don't deserve your success, just remember that you're no different than anyone else, including famous people throughout history. That should make you realize you're in good company even if you still have doubts about yourself.

Perhaps the best way to overcome your fear of being an imposter is to use your status as a success to help others. Actress Angelina Jolie has visited earthquake victims in Haiti and met with refugees from Kenya, Sri Lanka, and Jordan, earning her recognition as a UNHCR Goodwill Ambassador.

Bill Gates has given over $45 billion to a variety of charitable causes including controlling malaria and providing vaccines to control infectious diseases. Tennis superstar Serena Williams has donated money to help children in Kenya attend school for free.

No matter how much you may feel like an imposter due to your success, you can use your power, money, and status to help others. Whenever you help others, you'll find that you indirectly help yourself. So even if you still feel like a fraud, you can look at all the good you're doing and realize that it doesn't matter what others think just as long as you can continue doing good in this world.

FEAR OF YOURSELF

Ultimately, when people fear success, it's because they fear themselves. They fear how they might change in negative ways because they don't trust themselves to handle success well. If you don't believe you'll deal with success well, that's when you need to stop pursuing any goal and evaluate who you are as a person. Money doesn't make you happier, smarter, or better than anyone else. Money simply amplifies your personality for others to see.

One of the biggest NFL busts in history is Ryan Leaf, a quarterback who was chosen as the number two draft pick by the San Diego Chargers. Despite a successful college career where he was a finalist for the Heisman Trophy, Leaf racked up multiple losses in the NFL through his poor playing that he blamed on the media and his teammates.

He soon developed a reputation for a poor work ethic, such as playing golf while the other quarterbacks were studying film to improve their performance. General manager Bobby Beathard said this about Leaf: "Guys can be jerks, but I've never seen a guy that worked harder at alienating his teammates."

After the Chargers released him, Leaf tried to restart his career with several other teams but after continued poor play, he was soon out of the NFL for good. To this day, sportswriters and commentators have tagged potential quarterback flops in each year's draft as "the next Ryan Leaf."

Even after his football career was over, Leaf's problems didn't stop. He was indicted on burglary and controlled-substance charges in Texas, then arrested on burglary, theft, and drug charges in Montana a few years later.

Success didn't destroy Leaf. His own personality did. If he had never played in the NFL and never made millions of dollars, he would still have been a jerk. Having money and fame simply gave him more opportunities to show the world how immature and arrogant he really was.

If you're not a good person without money, you probably won't be a good person with money no matter how much you might have. Money doesn't mask your flaws; it highlights them.

If you're afraid of being exposed to the public, ask yourself: Why are you behaving in a potentially embarrassing manner in the first place? Rather than expend unnecessary energy trying to hide your flaws, it's far more beneficial to work on eliminating your flaws. The more open and honest you can be with yourself, the more open and honest you can be with others.

When the way you present yourself to others is exactly the same way you behave when you're alone, you'll have little to fear when you become a success because you won't have to change one bit.

SIGNS OF SELF-SABOTAGE

No matter what dreams you want to pursue, your biggest enemy will never be the economy, the political environment, the climate, or the law. Your biggest enemy will always be yourself. As long as you can overcome whatever limitations are stopping you, you'll be able to achieve anything you want.

What most people do is subconsciously sabotage their own success. This type of destructive self-sabotage can manifest in your life in several ways:

- Procrastination
- Perfectionism

- Low goals

- Quitting too soon

- Self-destructive behavior

Suppose you were dying of thirst in a desert and suddenly found a glass of water. Would you procrastinate about drinking it? Probably not. That's because when you want something badly enough, you'll take action to get it.

So when you procrastinate, that's a signal that even though you say you want something, there's something still stopping you. Procrastination can disguise itself by diverting your attention to other actions, many of which may even be important or necessary such as spending time with your loved ones or doing necessary chores such as emptying the trash. However the end result is that procrastination keeps you from actively progressing toward a specific goal that you want to achieve.

The key to procrastination is isolating the goal you want. First, ask yourself if you really want that goal. Sometimes you may want goals because other people want you to achieve them or because you think that's what you should pursue. If you don't want a goal, you'll find ways to avoid working toward it. In that case, you need to admit to yourself that you don't want that goal after all.

Sometimes you may even have a goal you want to achieve, but once you start pursuing it, you might realize it's not what you expected. In that case, it's perfectly fine to change your mind and pursue a more desirable goal. Just make sure you're really abandoning a goal because you no longer want it rather than giving up because you're discouraged by problems or obstacles in your way. Only you know for sure whether you're truly pursuing your passion or simply chasing after a frivolous idea just because the rewards seem appealing.

Procrastination can take on another form where you strive for perfection before moving forward. At all times, you definitely want to do the best you can, but you will never be perfect. The quest for perfection is just another form of procrastination where you think you can't move forward until you achieve something more – such as more education, more training, more practice, or more money. When you wait for everything to be perfect before you proceed, you'll be waiting forever and you will never proceed.

Strive for perfection but know you'll never achieve it. The perfect time will never arrive. Start where you are with what you have and learn as you go along. Waiting for perfection is another trap to keep you from risking failure. Once you realize it's okay to fail and not be perfect, you'll be able to move forward and overcome inevitable mistakes as they arise. When you pursue any goal, you will not know everything so you will make mistakes. Embrace those mistakes because each one moves you one step closer to your goal.

Professor Mason Cooley said, "Procrastination makes easy things hard, hard things harder." By finding the real reason you're procrastinating, you can answer the question why procrastinating is more appealing than pursuing your dreams.

Still another form of self-sabotage lies with choosing easily achievable goals. In movies, nobody cheers the hero when he or she parks a car. That's because that goal is too easy. Yet far too many people settle for choosing goals that are too low rather than chasing after grand ones. Setting a goal to double your income in one year is admirable. Setting a goal to earn an extra dollar a year is not. The higher the goals you set for yourself, the more exciting they will be to achieve.

Setting low goals that are somewhat of a stretch do have a purpose, though. They can define stepping stones you need to take to achieve your much bigger dreams. When you can achieve low goals consistently, then you'll develop the courage to start setting your sights higher. Someone trying to lose weight needs to start with an achievable goal at first, such as exercising daily to lose one pound in a week. Once they achieve that goal, they need to keep challenging themselves with bigger goals.

The only problem with choosing low goals is if you stop there. Use low goals to build your confidence and your consistency in achieving goals that you set for yourself. Then keep thinking bigger. Remember, every expert was a novice at one time, so there's no shame in setting low goals when you're first starting out. You just don't want to continue pursuing low goals forever.

Big goals are not easy to achieve. As a result, big goals means you'll need to face and overcome big problems. Unfortunately, you never know how many big problems you'll need to overcome until you finally reach your goal. All you know for sure is that the minute you stop overcoming problems and give up pursuing your goal, you'll never reach it.

In 2009, Jenn Hyman wanted to raise money for her business called Rent the Runway, where women could rent expensive dresses and have them delivered to their home. After wearing the dress, they could send it back and thereby get the chance to wear a fancy dress for a night or two at a fraction of the cost of buying that same dress.

Yet when Jenn and her co-founder, Jennifer Fleiss, went looking for venture capital, they ran into rich men who treated them arrogantly and condescendingly. Not only did these men not seriously consider their business as valid, but they also treated the two women as if they couldn't possibly be smart enough to run a business.

It wasn't until the two women set up pop-up shops and captured video of customers trying on fancy dresses and appearing with a greater sense of confidence that the *New York Times* published an article about their idea. That's when venture capital finally started to trickle in. If it hadn't been for their determination, their Rent the Runway business might have never become the $100 million success that it is today.

For several years, Stewart Butterfield tried to run a multi-player online game called Glitch, which he described as a combination of Dr. Seuss meets Monty Python. Although the game got good reviews and people signed up, players kept abandoning the game after only playing for a short time. That meant few players signed up to pay the monthly subscription fee and those that did quickly dropped out.

By 2012, Stewart concluded that Glitch was a failure and would have to be shut down. However, he realized that one key feature in Glitch that people seemed to like was its conversation-based communication system that players had used to chat with each other. Seeing the popularity of this communication tool, Stewart abandoned the gaming industry and focused his business on promoting this communication tool for others. In the process, he renamed his communication tool Slack, which became a multimillion dollar cloud-based collaboration business.

In 2020, Salesforce acquired Slack for $27.7 billion. The lesson is clear. The key to success in any goal lies in not quitting too soon. So the next time you feel discouraged and want to give up, realize just how close you might be from success if you only keep going.

Perhaps the most blatant forms of self-sabotage are your own habits. Are you taking care of your health? If you're not getting enough sleep, eating nutritious food, or exercising, you can't work at peak efficiency.

Beyond taking care of your health, how do your other habits help or hinder you? Are you chronically late? Do you procrastinate until the last second? Are you disorganized? Do you get along with others? Do you do your best at all times?

Examine your regular activities and see which ones are helping you and which ones are hurting you. You cannot drive fast in a car if you're pushing the accelerator and the brake at the same time. Likewise, you cannot progress easily toward your goals if you're sabotaging yourself at every step of the way.

With each activity and habit, ask yourself if it's helping you or hurting you. Then identify what benefit you receive through activities and habits that hurt you. There's always a reason why you do what you do, so it's crucial that you understand the reason why. Once you know what benefit you gain from destructive habits, then you can look for other ways to get that same benefit without that destructive habit. The goal is to replace self-sabotaging habits with more constructive ones.

Perhaps the most destructive behavior comes when you finally achieve everything you've ever dreamed about. As soon as you achieve your greatest dream, you might start wondering, "How can I ever repeat that same success again?"

The answer is simple. You don't. You embrace the activity that got you your dream.

Author Stephen King struggled to break into writing for years. When he finally completed his first novel, he threw it away because he didn't think it was any good. His wife retrieved it from the trash can and send it to a publisher, which accepted it. That first novel became a best seller named *Carrie*, which started Stephen King's prolific career.

After this first success, Stephen King could have worried that he would never write another best seller, but instead of worrying, he continued writing because his dream wasn't to write just one horror novel but to live a life where he could continue dreaming up new stories for people around the world to enjoy. While his initial dream was just to get a novel published, he expanded his dream to be able to support himself writing novels for the rest of his life. By pursuing a much larger dream, Stephen King remains one of the most prolific horror writers in the world.

Bethany Hamilton loved surfing. Unfortunately, when she was 13 years old, a shark attacked her and bit off her arm. Yet 26 days after she had lost two-thirds of her blood and nearly lost her life, Bethany was back on her surfboard. Two years later, she won a national championship.

Her goal wasn't just to win a surfing championship but to challenge herself, overcome the loss of her arm, and continue surfing because that's what she loves doing the most. When you focus on external rewards such as winning a championship, it's easy to doubt yourself and wonder if you can ever repeat your success again. However, when you embrace your passion, external rewards become far less important. Instead of striving for more external accolades, your passion will continue driving you to pursue the activity you enjoy the most.

By achieving massive success, you've proven you can do it. Now you can keep performing that same activity because you love it regardless of any external rewards.

Remember, the biggest obstacles to achieving any goal will always be you. If you can master yourself, you can achieve far more than you might have ever thought possible. You can achieve success as either a good person or a complete jerk. The choice is yours.

Just realize that whether you succeed or not, you'll always be the same person you've always been. If you're a good person before achieving success, you'll still be a good person after you achieve success. If you're an arrogant jerk before achieving success, you'll still be an arrogant jerk after achieving success.

Rather than worry about achieving material success, it's far more fruitful to work on creating a happy life filled with wonderful relationships of people you care about the most. Once you achieve that, any material success will just be a bonus. Don't fear success. Fear missing out on life because you forgot that your relationships with others and yourself is what truly matters in the end.

Takeaways: Fears can hold you back. The biggest obstacle to your success is always you. Success starts with little goals that let you achieve much bigger goals. By taking the first step to pursue your dreams, you're already a success.

THE ACTIVIST-PHYSICIST

By Gerald Fisher

Mario Savio is a good example of how good guys finish first. During the 1960s, he went to Mississippi to help African Americans register to vote. Then he taught at a freedom school for black children.

When he returned to Berkeley, he continued to fight against injustice. It was at the University of California–Berkeley where he made his speech known as "Operation of the Machine," where he said:

"There comes a time when the operation of the machine becomes so odious, makes you so sick at heart, that you can't take part! You can't even passively take part! And you've got to put your bodies upon the gears and upon the wheels . . . upon the levers, upon all the apparatus, and you've got to make it stop! And you've got to indicate to the people who run it, to the people who own it, that unless you're free, the machine will be prevented from working at all!"

Mario had the talent and ability to go to the very top of our profession, and had he done so, he would have been one of the very best examples of how the ultra best of the profession can also be among the ultra kind and gentle and supportive. He was an exemplary individual, and it was a pleasure for me to get to know him.

I had heard about him and seen him on the news many times during the free speech movement in Berkeley in the 1960s. When I saw his name on my appointment pad, I figured somebody might be making a joke, but when he showed up, I recognized him instantly.

He had been a physics and philosophy major, and now 15 years later, he wanted to finish his physics degree. So he asked me, "What do I have to do to enter the program?"

I told him, "You just did it."

He said, "Did what?"

I said, "You satisfied all the requirements that we have in the department for you to become a physics major."

He said, "I did nothing."

I said, "Those are the requirements."

Perplexed, he said, "Do I understand that the requirements to enter this department is to do nothing?"

"Exactly right," I said, "and you satisfied them with flying colors."

Before he could excuse himself and run out of the office, I smiled and decided to be a little more informative.

"Levity aside, there is one requirement to enter this department," I said. "You must be serious and have a reasonable chance of success."

(continued)

(*continued*)

Mario was grateful and showed it, and he was a sweet guy. He worked hard and he always had time for the other students, and he always was supportive. He was 10–15 years older than most of the students, maybe even more.

Once, the student body was talking about an event and Mario volunteered to be the host, spokesperson, and master of ceremonies. That's when one of the young women in the department turned to him and asked, "Have you ever spoken before in front of a large group?"

He didn't correct her or take any offense. He was just Mario, but he enhanced our whole department. Every class he was in, every meeting he had with students, just walking down the hallway saying hi, sent a little spark to everyone.

I didn't realize fully at the time, but people like that enhanced their environment and it is another example of how the premise of this book is all too true. Once sitting in the student union with Mario, someone came over and asked, "Are you Mario Savio?"

Mario replied, "Somebody has to be." Then he added, "Would you like to sit down?" He turned to me and asked, "Do you mind?"

I said no, it would be a great pleasure. Well, the three of us had a chat about the university and its pros and cons. That's the way Mario was. He had time for everybody.

In order for him to finish his degree, he had to take some necessary requirements, one of which was particularly stupid. They insisted that he take a California history course. Since Mario had helped shape California history in the 1960s, he should have been exempt from that class, but they made no exceptions.

I'm pretty convincing but I couldn't get him out of it. I even threatened to go to the governor. Finally I told him, "I think you're going to have to take the course."

So he said, "All right. I'll take it."

A month later, I was walking down the hallway and bumped into Mario and asked him, "How's the California history course going?"

He said, "Well, I was going to come see you about it because I'm really in a bind. Now in the class, we're talking about me. And frankly, the guy doesn't know crap about what happened in Berkeley in the 60s, and I don't know what to do. Should I drop the course?"

I said, "If you drop the course, you'll have to take it again. My advice to you is to stick with it. By the way, doesn't this instructor have a question about Mario Savio being on the enrollment sheet?"

Mario said, "Either he doesn't check or he thinks there's some kind of a gag, But anyway, it's never come up, and so you're advising me to stay with it?"

I said, "Yeah. Just stick with it." So Mario did stick with it and he got a B. For someone who helped shape California history during the 1960s, that's like Mozart getting a B in music composition or Shakespeare getting a B in literature.

Mario went on to finish his bachelor's degree with honors. Two years later, he received his master's of physics

(*continued*)

(*continued*)

with his thesis being awarded as the outstanding master's thesis in the entire university. The administration of the university had a general philosophy that they would take credit for what they had nothing to do with. So the dean and the president went on stage and announced the award. Mario stood up, got emotional, thanked us and the department, and said how grateful he was. He got a standing ovation. While everyone sat back down, I started walking down the center aisle toward the stage.

Mario caught my eye and walked off the stage, down the stairs, and started walking up the aisle that I was coming down. Everyone on the stage just stared at the two of us as I spread out my arms to full wing span. Mario did the same, and when we met about halfway up the aisle we both instinctively embraced.

We both started to cry. I slapped him on the back and he kissed my cheek. Then I sent him back up on the stage. It was just a wonderful feeling.

That was Mario. He was a great guy, and his kindness elevated everyone in the department. When I look at what Mario accomplished both inside the physics department and outside, I'm convinced that nice guys can and do finish first every time.

CHAPTER 11

Achieving Your Dream

Ten years from now, you'll be 10 years older, no matter what you do. If you do nothing more than what you're doing right now, you'll just have more of what you see in front of you. If you're happy with that, there's no reason to change or try anything different.

However, if you want something else, then you need to ask yourself where do you want to be in the future? Think of how much different a newborn toddler looks today than he or she will look 10 years from now. Each year, you may notice gradual changes as a child grows up, but after 10 years, you'll see a dramatic difference.

That's how you have to see your own life. Year by year, the changes may seem minor and inconsequential, but after 5 or 10 years, you'll see tremendous changes. Since you'll be 10 years older 10 years from now, the key is deciding where you want to be in those 10 years.

You can and will succeed in one form or another. If you define a goal and work toward it, you're already a success regardless of what anyone else might think. Success is never about a fixed outcome but how you actively choose to live your own life.

While writing this book, my good friend and colleague for over 23 years passed away. Dr. James A. Redfield had a heart attack while biking and was found unresponsive. Despite having his life cut short far sooner than anyone thought possible, Dr. Redfield spent every day living life to its fullest. Just days before his fatal heart attack, he had written me an inspiring letter looking forward to the future:

> *Dear Jon,*
>
> *I write to you as a dedicated friend for over 20 years as we near the final stages of our development together at CrowdOptic.*
>
> *I believe that here at CrowdOptic we have created one of the most obvious and beneficial products designed specifically for health sciences. The product we created at Bharosa [purchased by Oracle and now used by Wells Fargo] saved money.*
>
> *Our CrowdOptic product saves lives. Big difference.*
>
> *I believe this life-saving technology is the best culmination of our work while over 20 years together.*
>
> *There is little time to be wasted and huge benefits to be realized. Good luck with our march forward. Let's finish this soon.*

Keep in mind that happiness is more than just achieving specific goals. Life is a journey that you never know might suddenly end or go long into the future. Every day, ask yourself, "If this were the last time I would see people around me, how do I want to treat them and have them remember me?"

Did you hug your child today and let him or her know how much you love them? Did you kiss your partner today and let them know how much they mean to you? Did you talk to a friend and let them know how much you treasure their friendship? Have you stayed in touch with distant friends and relatives to let them know they're still part of your life? Are you kind to strangers? What would be the last memory you'd want others to think of you? When you know that, go out and make sure you bring those memories to life.

Life is like a roller coaster with its ups and downs. Sometimes life might seem to be working against you and sometimes it might seem out of your control, but no matter what happens, you can always control how you react to adversity. The most powerful person in the world is one who knows they're in control of their life.

Jane Wiedlin, guitarist for The Go-Go's, the only all-woman band to write and play their own songs that topped the Billboard music charts, said (https://www.retrojunk.com/article/show/3268/a-talk-with-jane-wiedlin), "I thought life was completely pointless when I was in high school, but just a few short years later I was having the adventure of a lifetime in a successful rock band!"

Happiness requires you to take constant action performing an activity that brings you joy. Happiness is an experience you share with others to create happy memories that can last a lifetime. Happiness is the satisfaction you feel when you know you've poured your heart and soul into a purpose. Happiness is within your reach, starting now.

You have everything you need to be happy and live a wonderful life. The first step is to believe that your life can change for the better. The second step is to identify your passion. The third step is to define a goal that lets you pursue your passion. The fourth step is to share your passion with those around you. Happiness is never an isolated emotion but a shared experience. The happiest people are those who spread their joy to others.

We may never meet in person, but through this book, I trust we've been able to connect emotionally, intellectually, and spiritually. If you remember nothing else from this book, remember this: Believe in yourself and never give up. You are greater than you think. You can achieve wonderful things if you only try. You are unique because there's only one person exactly like you with your distinctive gifts and viewpoint to share with the world.

Johann Wolfgang von Goethe said, "Whatever you do, or dream you can, begin it. Boldness has genius and power and magic in it."

So what are you waiting for? Why don't you get started?

Takeaways: Relish every moment, because you never know how much time you have on Earth. You hold the power to control and change your life for the better. The big question isn't what can you do, but when are you going to start doing it?

THE IMMIGRANT

By Gerald Fisher

I've known many wonderful scientists and scholars. However, this last person was not a scientist. Not only did he not get an advanced degree, but he didn't even get into college and may have only gone up to the sixth or eighth grade.

Louis was born in Galecia in the 1880s, which has always been described to me as a small section between Lithuania and Poland. Louis entered into an arranged marriage at the age of 16. His bride was 15. They didn't know what marriage was all about. They thought it was a tradition where the oldest son got married off to the oldest daughter of another family and set up a household.

After a year or two and some prodding from their relatives, they learned about marriage, and there soon followed one son and one daughter. In 1910, Louis thought they should all go to America and have a new life, but he couldn't afford a trip for anyone but himself.

It's not clear how he got to the coast; nor do we know anything about the steamer that took him across the Atlantic. Somehow, he managed to fulfill his dream of coming to the United States.

He worked hard, saved every penny, would go to the automat, fill up a bowl with hot water, sit down at a table, put ketchup in it, and make homemade tomato soup. That was his zero-cost dinner.

When he had saved up enough money, he brought over his pregnant wife and his two kids in 1911. My father was born that year, and two more kids followed in short order. Louis Fisher was my grandfather.

He was just a wonderful American. My grandmother once told me that she only knew of two times in his entire life that Grandpa cried. The first time was when the ship entered New York harbor after the long trip. When it sailed past the Statue of Liberty, grandpa couldn't hold back the tears.

The second time he cried was 12 years later, when he became an American citizen. He described it as the proudest day of his life.

When I was 13 years old, I got arrested. I tried to explain the situation to my grandpa but couldn't. I wasn't too surprised, because at that age I thought I knew everything, and one of those things that was absolutely clear to me was that my grandfather was the stupidest man on Earth.

It was an air raid drill; we refused to take cover. "Why didn't you take cover?" he asked.

(*continued*)

(*continued*)

I said, "It's ridiculous because if a nuclear bomb goes off, they would find all these people ducking under chairs, in basements and subways, cremated in place."

He didn't get it. My father was standing off in the corner smiling. I took his smile as a confirmation of the brilliance of my argument, but in retrospect, with 60+ years of additional contemplation, I must admit that Dad probably knew exactly what was going on.

Finally, Grandpa seemed to understand, and said, "Let me understand this. You refused to take cover when ordered by the police?"

I said, "That's right, Grandpa." My grandpa looked at me, smirked, and said, "You know, I thank God Almighty for this wonderful country, where a schmuck like you can defy the police and not get his head bashed in."

Over time, I gradually came to realize just how smart and perceptive my grandfather really was. Unfortunately, he didn't live long enough for me to tell him. My father told me once that he was sure that Grandpa knew how I really felt, but I still wish I could have told him how smart he really was, given him a hug, and told him how much I appreciated what he did for us and how much I loved him.

When he was studying to take the citizenship exam, he was working hard. He took book after book out of the library to study late into the night. Finally, my father and his brothers and sisters all got together to emphasize that he did not have to work so hard.

Grandpa said he knew that the exam would not be challenging, but that was not the point. He was working so hard and putting in such long hours so that he could be the greatest and best citizen candidate that the country ever witnessed.

The morning of the exam, he went to the barber shop for a professional shave because everything had to be perfect. When he returned home, he put on his only suit that he had cleaned twice. My father said that when the examiner called his name, he became so nervous that he thought they would have to postpone the proceedings, but Grandpa gathered his wits about him and passed. When he was sworn in as the newest citizen of the United States of America, that was when the tears began to flow.

1888 was the year another immigrant was born. His name was Issur Baylene, and he came with his parents from Russia when he was four years old. He also loved this country immensely, and when he was still a teenager, he changed his name to Irving Berlin.

In 1918, he used his incredible talent to show how he felt about his country by writing "God Bless America." To my mind, that is the greatest musical work ever produced. I guess I inherited something from my granddad, because whenever that song is played, I have a very hard time holding back the tears.

Finally, I would like to say thanks to the grandfather of the majority leader of the US Senate, Chuck Schumer. His grandpa also came from Galecia, also had a profound feeling of gratitude to the wonderful country that took him in, and passed it on to his son. Chuck Schumer's middle name is Ellis, named after Ellis Island. Chuck Schumer

(continued)

(*continued*)

even gave his daughter the middle name of Emma, after Emma Lazarus, who wrote those immortal words, "Give me your tired, your poor, your huddles masses yearning to breathe free."

I hope to meet Senator Schumer some day to compare notes about the immigrants – our fathers and grandfathers – who all shared a love for this wonderful country. If that takes place, as I hope it does one day, I'll share what my own grandfather must have felt when he saw the Statue of Liberty for the first time and realized the hope it held for the future of everyone who came to this country in search of a better life.

ABOUT THE AUTHORS

Jon Fisher is a Silicon Valley entrepreneur, investor, author, speaker, philanthropist, and inventor. Fisher is known for advocating start-up acquisition strategy versus an IPO and is the author of *Strategic Entrepreneurism: Shattering the Start-Up Entrepreneurial Myths.*

Jon is a recipient of the Ernst & Young Entrepreneur of the Year Award (Emerging Category, 2007), and is a prolific inventor, named on more than 100 patents issued and pending worldwide. Jon spoke of a path of least resistance building software companies in a University of San Francisco commencement address, which has been viewed more than 6 million times and will be the subject of a book by John Wiley & Sons, Inc. coming in the fall of 2021. Artwork of Jon's speech sold at auction as the 89th most valuable NFT on April 29, 2021. Jon serves on the Democratic National Committee's national finance team. Jon lives in Marin County, California, with his wife and daughter.

Gerald A. Fisher has been an active member of the nuclear physics community for over 50 years. After graduating with a B.S. in Physics and Mathematics from the City College of New York, he received his PhD in nuclear physics from Stanford University. As a visiting professor, he did research in the field of nuclear physics and taught at Stanford University. At San Francisco State University, he worked as the department head of physics for 20 years.

Wallace Wang has written over 50 books, including *Microsoft Office for Dummies, Steal This Computer Book*, and co-authored *Strategic Entrepreneurism* and *Breaking into Acting for Dummies*. When he's not teaching iPhone programming and game design, he blogs about screenwriting at his site, the 15 Minute Movie Method (www.15minutemoviemethod.com), where he shares tips about story structure and scene writing for screenplays. He also runs the Cat Daily News (www.catdailynews.com) website for cat enthusiasts.